Naked With Only the Will to Survive

Naked With Only the Will to Survive

...

Johnny Adams and Kim Adams Graham

ISBN: 1981274901
ISBN-13: 9781981274901
Library of Congress Control Number: 2017918711
CreateSpace Independent Publishing Platform
North Charleston, South Carolina

Contents

Introduction

• • •

Lisa Joy Theris is a beautiful twenty-five-year-old woman who lives in Louisville, Alabama. She has long, wavy brown hair; bright-blue eyes; and an olive complexion. She is intelligent, witty, and a joy to be around. She makes friends easily.

Growing up, she had the most wonderful life any child could ask for, but she tainted her early teenage years with alcohol and excessive Xanax use. After graduating high school, she escalated her drug use.

She moved to Tuscaloosa, Alabama; then to Mobile, Alabama; and eventually to Corpus Christi, Texas. She began using different types of drugs, and as her drug lifestyle progressively became worse and worse, she made increasingly bad decisions and ended up in an abusive relationship. When things went bad in Lisa's life, she moved back home to Louisville, Alabama, when she was twenty-four years old.

For several months, Lisa had her life back on track and was doing great. She was attending college and making good grades, and she was drug-free. Sadly, that didn't last very long. She met new friends and began using drugs again.

She would stay awake for days at a time. Eventually, while hanging out with the wrong crowd, she rode with one of her friends to a hunting lodge located in a rural area. Lisa thought a friend and another person were going to break in to the hunting lodge and while she believed a burglary was in progress, she became frightened and hid in the woods.

As her anxiety intensified, Lisa began to fear for her life and went deeper into the woods, soon becoming hopelessly lost. She spent twenty-five days in the woods with no food, no clothes—nothing. Lisa was totally naked, and the only thing she had was a will to survive. This book gives details of Lisa Joy Theris's life story, including her near-death experience of being lost in the woods for twenty-five days.

Lisa survived, and she wants the readers of this book to know how drugs led her down a bad path that almost led to her death.

Timeline

• • •

1975—William and Joanne Theris marry

June 25, 1992—Lisa Joy Theris is born in Puyricard, France

1999—Lisa moves to America

May 2010—Lisa graduates from Ariton High School

June 2010—Lisa begins Enterprise Community College

January 2011—Lisa moves to Tuscaloosa, Alabama

September 2011—Lisa moves to Mobile, Alabama

September 2011–July 2016—Lisa works at Hooters

July 2016–August 2016—Lisa is in Texas

January 2017—Lisa begins Wallace Community College

May 2017—Lisa meets Richard.

June 2017—Lisa is charged with disorderly conduct in Coffee County, Alabama

June 2017—Lisa begins her second semester at Wallace Community College

July 9, 2017—Lisa is in a terrible car wreck in Georgia

July 18, 2017—Lisa's father has his last contact with Lisa, the lodge is allegedly burglarized, and Lisa is forced to enter the woods

July 23, 2017—Lisa's father and two friends report Lisa missing to the Troy Police Department, and an investigation begins

July 31, 2017—Richard John Jefferson is arrested

August 2, 2017—The search begins with personnel from Bullock County Sheriff's Department, Alabama Department of Conservation, Easterling Correctional Facility, Troy Police Department, Clayton Police Department, Pike County Sheriff Dive Team, Ventress Correctional Facility, K-9 Specialty from Columbiana, Tallaco K-9 from Dadeville, and employees from the State Land Division

August 4, 2017—George Lee Harvey is arrested

August 10, 2017—Lisa's charges are dropped in Coffee County

August 12, 2017—Around 2:00 p.m., Lisa Joy Theris is found alive

Notice

• • •

<small>Some of the names have</small> been changed in this book to protect them and their reputations. A few—including but not limited to—Maxine, Habitha, Bent, Lenard, Ronald, George Lee Harvey and Richard John Jefferson—are the products of the authors' imaginations and have been substituted for real names. Any resemblance of these names to actual persons, living or dead, is purely coincidental. Only the names have been changed; all events described in this book, including the events relating to those names, are believed to be true and accurate. However, some events are based upon the memories of events which the persons involved can differ. This book is not intended to hurt anyone. As of the publication of this book, the burglary and theft charges mentioned herein have not been dismissed nor have they been confirmed by a jury. The persons actually charged with burglary and theft are innocent until proven guilty.

Lisa Spends Early Years in France

• • •

Lisa Joy Theris was born in Puyricard, France, on June 25, 1992, to William and Joanne Theris.

She has three sisters: Rebecca "Becky" Theris of Boston, Massachusetts; Angelina Theris Owens of Gainesville, Florida; and Elizabeth "Lizzy" Theris of Pensacola, Florida. She also has six brothers: Robert and William Theris, both of Mobile, Alabama; Jonathan "Johnny" Theris of Boston; Christopher Theris of Paris, France; Nathaniel "Nate" Theris of Providence, Rhode Island; and Emmanuel "Eman" Theris of Mobile, Alabama.

Lisa has four half brothers and one half sister. Lisa's father had one child by Kathy Salas, a son named Michael Salas of Narragansett, Rhode Island. Kathy still lives in France, and Lisa calls her Aunt Kathy. Lisa's father also has four children by Marie Christine De Micas of Martigues, France, including three sons (Guillaume, Johnny, and Nicolas De Micas) and one daughter (Marianne De Micas), all of Martigues. Marie still lives in Martigues and is known to the younger Theris children as Aunt Rose, which is the name she was given during her time as a member of the religious movement called "the Family." The movement was founded by David Berg in California in the 1960s and has now been renamed "the Family International."

Lisa Theris and her brother Mikey Salas

Lisa Theris and her brother Nick DeMicas

Giulluame DeMicas, Johnny DeMicas, Lisa Theris,
Lizzy Theris and Will Theris

Marianne DeMicas and Lisa Theris

Lizzy, Lisa, Joanne and William Theris

Lisa's parents, William and Joanne Theris, have been married since 1975 and joined the Family as missionaries before she was born. During their marriage, while in the religious movement, William formed two other families with Aunt Kathy and Aunt Rose. They all lived together in one home and were one big happy family, according to Lisa and her parents.

William and Joanne believed the movement was about bringing people to Jesus, loving your neighbor, doing well by others, and all the other good qualities many people associate with Christianity. In reality, this group was a religious cult. The movement kept its members isolated, taught distrust of the outside world, and grew its numbers by using sex to gain members, a practice playfully named "flirty fishing."

Cult leader David Berg derived the term "flirty fishing" from Matthew 4:19 from the New Testament, in which Jesus tells two fishermen that he will make them "fishers of men." Berg extrapolated from this that women in his movement should be "flirty fishers" (also called "bait" or "fisherwomen"), whereas the targeted men were called "fish." The cult published several documents with exact instructions, defining flirty fishing as using sex appeal for proselytizing. The Family International ended this practice in 1987, and according to some sources, hundreds of thousands of men were "fished" before the practice was discontinued.

In order to solidify indoctrination, members of the movement were not allowed to have contact with anyone outside the cult. It was later revealed that many of the children in this cult were being sexually abused. Lisa maintains that she and her siblings were never sexually abused, but this did often occur in different groups among the "higher-ups," the homes at the top of the Family hierarchy with the most power and control. From talking with her older siblings about their time in the Family, Lisa gathers that most of their memories are positive.

When the Therises realized what kinds of things were taking place, they left the cult and began traveling throughout France. William has always been a jack-of-all-trades and supported the family through various jobs, including carpentry and construction. Almost ten years after leaving the Family, William decided that it was time for the Therises to move back to the States. They continued to have a close relationship with Aunt Kathy, Aunt Rose, and their children, but needless to say, this was a difficult separation.

Lisa Theris' grandmother Doris

William moved to the United States ahead of Joanne and the children and began remodeling the Theris home in Louisville, Alabama, the house in which his mother, Doris, had been born. Lisa's grandmother, Doris Donaldson Theris, is a wonderful woman who grew up in Louisville. She was once selected as Miss Peanut in a pageant in Dothan, Alabama, and has participated in and won numerous beauty pageants. She has always enjoyed watching the Atlanta Braves baseball games and remains one of their biggest fans. She was married to William "Jeep" Theris. He played football for the University of Alabama. He also served the country in the US Army and played for an army football team. He died from cancer, and sadly, Lisa never met him. All Joanne Theris' family lived in New York, including Lisa's grandfather, Bernard, who she was particularly fond of.

Lisa Theris' grandfather Jeep

Grandfather Bernard and Theris children

After the home had been remodeled, Joanne and all their children, except Christopher, moved to the United States. Already studying to become an attorney, Chris was encouraged by his father to stay in France and pursue his career. Nate and Eman (Lisa's oldest brother) had traveled to the States ahead of the rest of the family and were already living in Mobile, Alabama. Christopher continues to reside in France and is a successful attorney with a beautiful family.

Lizzy, Becky, Rob, Chris, Marianne and Lisa

Lisa remembers that the four youngest children, herself included, were very excited about moving to America. Her dad had told them that in the United States, there were all-you-can-eat buffets, a previously unheard-of and unimagined concept. Equally intriguing was the idea of fried chicken. Her father had described beautiful, pristine beaches and pleasantly warm weather, and the children were thrilled, imagining all the adventures that awaited them.

Her older siblings, on the other hand, were not in the least bit excited about moving. All their friends were in France. They had a whole life they would be leaving behind, not to mention the culture shock. A few weeks after arriving in Alabama, Becky decided to move north, another distressing separation for Lisa. Becky was the oldest of the girls and had always taken care of them and added an element of whimsy to their lives. Lizzy has often waxed nostalgic about the time Becky stuck raisins in between Lisa's toes when she was little, and while this may have caused Lisa to cry at the time, Lizzy assures her that if she had been old enough to remember, it would be a treasured memory.

Lisa was seven years old when she moved to "America the Beautiful," and she says she could not have been happier.

The Theris Family's first day in the United States

In an effort to become a part of the community, the children began attending Louisville Baptist Church. The boys, Will and Rob, stopped going after about one year, in revolt against being asked to play with puppets during the Wednesday-night children's service. Lizzy and Lisa attended church twice a week for about six years. They loved going to church camp every year, and Lisa was so touched at one of the camps that she decided to be baptized after returning home. She enjoyed participating in the church plays and singing, and sometimes she would do interpretive movement while lip-synching. Attending church gave Lisa feelings of comfort and community, and she remembers those days fondly.

Lisa Theris and Lizzy Theris on Easter Sunday

Lisa's School Years

• • •

LISA ATTENDED KINDERGARTEN AND FIRST grade in France. She learned English at home and picked up the French language by being surrounded by it in school, sink-or-swim style. Her first day of school was rather memorable, for both her and the teacher. Lisa and her mom were both crying because they didn't want to be separated, and a kindly man came out of the building to see if he could help ease the transition. Lisa remembers struggling with and kicking him, causing a big scene. That man turned out to be the kindergarten teacher and ended up being one of Lisa's favorites.

Lisa Theris at her 4th birthday party

Despite the dramatic kickoff, Lisa has wonderful memories of her school in France. When she was only four years old, she went on a school trip to a farm for a week, where she learned how to milk cows and make cheese. She and her class would also go on weekly field trips to museums and to the pool for swimming lessons. They had a gymnastics room equipped with everything you could imagine, and Lisa was also able to take dance lessons.

Lisa Theris in participating in a school play

Recess was Lisa's favorite time of the day. Her brother Robert, who was about three grades ahead of Lisa, had recess at the same time as her. Lisa was a tomboy at that age and would play tag with Robert and his friends. She could run very fast and loved showing it. Several long-suffering sighs and irritated looks later, she realized Rob didn't like her playing with him and his friends, so she stopped and began doing the same thing the other students in her class would do: stand around and gossip.

Lisa Theris and Rob Theris at his high school graduation

As with many children her age, another of Lisa's favorite times of day was lunchtime. While the school did give the children the option to go home for lunch, where they would eat the types of food they were more accustomed to, they also enjoyed occasionally eating at the school cafeteria. Here they would sample, with no little trepidation, more unusual foods, such as cow tongue or boudin (blood sausage).

Not only the food in France but also the culture itself and the attitudes toward certain things were vastly different from what they are here in the States. Alcohol laws, for example, were much more laid back. There was nothing strange about a child purchasing wine from the store, though it was obviously presumed to be for the parents.

Nudity was also not viewed as severely, though this was a cultural difference with which Lisa was not comfortable. Every Monday, Lisa's class would go to the swimming pool. This was an outing that Lisa dreaded, because the boys and girls, due to their young age, would change clothes in the same locker room. While everyone acted like it was normal, Lisa always thought it was quite strange and kept her bathing suit on under her clothes. Even after swimming class, she would put her clothes back on over her wet swimming suit, despite her teacher's attempts at enforcing the rules.

Once a year, the entire school had a Mardi Gras carnival. All the students dressed up in masks and costumes they handmade in class and paraded through the streets, playing instruments and making merry. These were some of Lisa's favorite memories.

Another of Lisa's most treasured memories is when she and her family lived at the Boulet. Her family moved around every few years, and Lisa liked all the places they lived, but the Boulet was incomparable. She was only two or three years old at the time and just starting prekindergarten. The property was beautiful. It had cherry and apple trees and a huge garden filled with all kinds of marvelous flowers. It had a lake that would freeze over in the wintertime, and her dad would put her in a bucket and swing her around with a rope attached, while she laughed herself breathless.

Moving to the United States was quite a change. Lisa remembers stepping off the airplane and feeling the heat and high humidity. Her aunt Angie picked her and her family up at the airport in Atlanta, Georgia, and took them to their new home in Louisville, Alabama.

Lisa began attending Louisville Elementary School (LES). The education system in France had been advanced, and so Lisa's education in America began with topics she had already learned, which helped with the transition. She completed the second, third, and fourth grades at LES and then was homeschooled by her mother in the fifth grade. She attended Dixie Academy in the sixth grade, where she was selected Dixie Doll in a pageant. She attended Ariton Public School in the seventh grade and remained there until graduating high school. Lisa was an A student in elementary school, and her grades continued to be good through high school, where she took advanced classes.

Lisa Theris holding a sports trophy

Lisa was a very energetic and active child and enjoyed playing various sports, mostly at home with her brothers and sister, including basketball, baseball, rugby, soccer, badminton, and tennis. Lisa and her brother Robert were always on a team together, with Lizzy and Will on the other team. While it was certainly all for the pursuit of fun, they took their games very seriously. During their basketball "season," Will kept up a notebook for each player's stats for rebounds, steals, and fouls. And fouls there were aplenty. Lisa was aggressively defensive while playing basketball, and once Lizzy snapped and shoved Lisa away from her with all the frustrated strength of an angry twelve-year-old. Lisa flew across the court and off into the bushes, giving Lizzy a few stunned moments to bask in the glow of her accomplishment, quickly followed by the dismayed realization of what was to come. Sure enough, Lisa jumped up with the fury of wounded pride and skinned palms and came after Lizzy with her fists swinging. The two were eventually pulled apart by Will and Rob and temporarily benched for disorderly conduct. Just another short-lived explosion of temper, this soon blew over, and the girls went back to being the closest of companions.

Lisa enjoyed playing volleyball at Ariton High School. She also enjoyed attending football games, basketball games, volleyball games, and spending time with friends; she describes herself as an ordinary teenager.

Lisa Theris High School Volleyball picture

Growing up, she always got along with everyone. She disliked bullying and always treated everyone equally. While in school or at work, Lisa befriended all manner of personalities—the popular, the more reserved, and also those always managing to get into trouble. In fact, Lisa herself seemed to get in trouble often.

Trouble seemed to find Lisa even when she was not looking for it. She was rebuked by teachers on a regular basis for not following the school dress code, like wearing blue jeans with holes in the knees, wearing tank tops, and wearing shirts that would expose her stomach when she raised her arms.

When she was in the seventh grade, she was suspended for going into the boys' bathroom on a dare and knocking on each stall. Lisa did not anticipate such a severe punishment for this minor misconduct, as there hadn't even been anyone in the stalls. It is worth wondering whether the blind enforcement of rules for the sake of their existence, without the presence of harm done, contributes to a lack of respect for any kind of structured system at all.

One of the most serious transgressions that Lisa committed in school was starting a fight in the lunchroom. A classmate was angry and jealous of Lisa's friendship with her boyfriend, though any nonplatonic feelings were completely one-sided and unrequited on Lisa's part. Nonetheless, when Lisa confronted the girl, things became heated, and they began fighting. During the fight, Lisa accidentally struck a teacher in his nose while he was trying to break the two girls up. This man was one of Lisa's favorite teachers, and she has always regretted this incident.

Lisa began drinking alcohol when she was about twelve years old, given to her by some of her older friends from school.

As Lisa grew older herself, she began to skip school and get into trouble more often. She was frequently sent to Principal/ Coach Herring's office. He was very understanding and always gave her good advice when she got into trouble, which made her feel even worse for letting him down. Lisa could tell he actually cared about his job and his students, but she was headstrong and seemed to have an aversion to following rules. Lisa was never a perfect angel; she always had a little wild streak.

Lisa began to date and had her first real boyfriend during her tenth-grade year. This is when she decided to try methamphetamine (meth) for the first time. When her boyfriend was not on meth, he was the perfect guy. However, when he was on meth, he didn't care about anything.

Soon Lisa wanted to feel like him and not care about anything either. Her boyfriend let her try what she thought was meth one night. She later found out she had snorted some type of crushed pills, which had no effect on her. Lisa never understood why her boyfriend thought it was acceptable for him to do meth, but not her. She now believes he really didn't want her to do meth because he didn't want her to go down a bad path.

Not one to be easily discouraged once she made up her mind, Lisa obtained meth for herself. She and a friend tried it for the first time, snorting a tiny line each. Lisa hated it. She felt weird and paranoid, and the next day she and the friend felt worse than they ever had in their lives. The two lay in bed all day long. After that first try, she left meth alone for a long time; it wasn't the drug for her, and neither was her boyfriend. In the eleventh grade, she and a friend began skipping school on a regular basis to go snort cocaine and drink alcohol. Lisa's parents tried to convince her to enter a rehab program, but she refused.

During Lisa's senior year of high school, she was taking Lortab and Xanax, but nothing harder than that. That school year, she had settled down a lot. She was usually at school or spending time with a new boyfriend. Her boyfriend asked her to marry him, and

Lisa agreed. He joined the army and moved to Hawaii, and their engagement continued as a long-distance relationship. They eventually split up because Lisa didn't want to move to Hawaii; they never married. Lisa maintained good grades and graduated from Ariton High School in May of 2010.

Lisa Theris receives high school diploma
from Principal Ben Baker.

After High School

. . .

AFTER HIGH SCHOOL, LISA BEGAN college at Enterprise State Community College in Enterprise, Alabama, in June of 2010. She was working on a nursing degree and attended that school for about one year. She attended every class and made good grades. But something was missing; she felt bored. She wanted a change and felt like a larger city would be more exciting, so she moved to Tuscaloosa, Alabama.

She moved into an apartment with her sister Lizzy, who was already living there. On a fortunate stroke of serendipity, Lizzy had recently gone through a breakup and had an extra bedroom available. Lisa began attending Shelton State Community College in Tuscaloosa, Alabama. She was still studying in the field of nursing, while Lizzy went to the University of Alabama for her master's degree in library science.

She and Lizzy made great memories while living together and also made lifelong friends while in Tuscaloosa. Lisa was on a good path; everything was going great until she started working at the Waffle House located on the Strip. Most of the employees were young and attractive. The Waffle House was located near bars and clubs, which led to good tips from people leaving those businesses late at night. She usually worked from 6:00 p.m. until 6:00 a.m.

While working there, she met a friend and began going to parties and using various drugs, including psychedelics such as LSD.

Lisa was back on the wrong path in life. Her parents knew she was making bad decisions and convinced her and Lizzy to move to Mobile, Alabama, with their brother Nate in September 2012.

This was one of the happiest time periods of Lisa's life. Nate had been gone for a very long time, and even though through her childhood she had very few memories with him, she felt just as close to him as her siblings she had grown up with. She and Nate had written letters back and forth to each other through all those years. When the three of them moved in together and were able to spend time with one another, it really meant a lot to him. Lisa also loved being roommates with Lizzy. They were both excited to have their very own place, Yester Oakes Apartments in Mobile, Alabama. The only problem for Lisa and Lizzy was their work shifts were different, so they didn't see each other as much as they wished. Lisa was very sad when Lizzy moved in with her boyfriend, because she was so attached to Lizzy and could not imagine seeing her less. Lizzy was very intelligent and moved away from home at fourteen years old to attend the Alabama School of Mathematics and Science in Mobile, Alabama. So they saw each other only on holidays or when Lisa would go visit Lizzy at her school. Also, Will moved to Rhode Island during this time because the country just wasn't his scene. This left Lisa and Robert, her youngest brother, in Louisville. She and Robert were the closest siblings because of this. They did everything together. Everyone they met thought they were twins even though he was a few years older than her. He was very protective of Lisa. When he found out she stayed at a boy's house for the first time, he stopped talking to Lisa for months. Lisa did not like the fact that she and her brother were not talking. He was her best friend, but they were both so stubborn, and neither of them would break the ice. It wasn't until Will and Lizzy came home to visit that they broke the silence while having some drinks together. Neither one has ever brought up the subject again.

Working at Hooters

• • •

Lisa moved in with Nate in September 2012 with the intention of enrolling at the University of South Alabama in Mobile, Alabama. She never enrolled, however, and began working at Hooters.

Hooters Girls - Paige, Tari and Lisa

Shortly after arriving in Mobile, Lisa rode by Hooters on Airport Boulevard and decided to fill out a job application there.

She had an interview and was hired that same day. Lisa said all the girls who had worked there for a while were petty toward the new girls. That was just the way it was. After Lisa talked to the manager about her new position, she overheard some of the girls telling another Hooters girl named Paige that Lisa looked like she could be her twin. Paige did not like hearing that another female looked like her and replied, "No, the hell she doesn't." Lisa laughed in her head, thinking that was exactly what *she* would have said too.

It took them a while, but she and Paige became friends. To this day, they call each other "sister" or "twin." She is still one of Lisa's closest friends, along with many other Hooters girls.

Lisa Theris and friends

While working at Hooters, Lisa noticed there were more families eating in the restaurant than single men. Also, a lot of men would take their dates to Hooters, which Lisa found counterintuitive. Why would any girl want to be taken to a Hooters restaurant on a date? On Valentine's Day, it would get crazy because of a special sale Hooters would always offer: buy ten wings and get ten free. The place would be so packed they would have to turn some customers away.

Lisa felt that some people looked down on Hooters girls because of their uniforms. Lisa did not understand the problem with the uniforms: just a tank top, shorts, long white socks, and tennis shoes.

Most people probably did not know that Hooters had uniform checks every day before the shift started. If the shorts were too short or showed too much of the girls' cheeks, they would not be allowed on the floor until they changed into a larger size. The shirts had to be perfectly clean and bright white; anything less and you would be forced to replace it.

According to Lisa, the biggest problem for the Hooters girls was the shoes. They cost about fifty dollars and had to be cleaned before the shift started. The managers would also check the Hooters girls' mouths and ears to make sure there were no piercings except for the one pair of stud earrings they were allowed. All tattoos had to be covered with makeup. Lisa had to wear a bandage over her nose ring for a while. She finally grew tired of the bandage and just took the nose ring out and let the hole close. Hooters girls had to wear their hair down and styled at all times. Too much makeup was not tolerated; all makeup had to look natural, but at the same time, not wearing makeup was unacceptable.

Management would take a picture of each Hooters girl at the time she was hired. If a Hooters girl gained too much weight and looked different from the picture, she could be fired. Gym memberships, saunas, and a girls-only weight room were available to the Hooters girls so they could stay in shape.

Of course, there was always drama at Hooters; how could there not be with one building and so many young women? The

Hooters girls would argue over which sections they would work and who would get to go home early during early cuts.

Lisa said the kitchen crew at Hooters was amazing. They always kept the girls laughing—if they were not mad at them for bringing back food that the customer thought was not properly prepared.

Management was great for the most part; they were not only bosses but friends too. It was like a big family. Lisa worked there for four years and became very attached to her coworkers.

Hooters is like no other job that Lisa will ever have again. On good nights, she would make around $150; on a double shift, she would make up to $300; and on a slow night, she would make around $80.

Silly little games were played to pick the sections they would work. But they were fun games, and Lisa was pretty good at them, such as who could spit croutons the farthest and who could throw mayo packets closest to the bucket and then ring the bucket to get a free meal. They also competed to see who could kick, roll, or throw a paper towel roll the farthest. Most of the time, they would see who could toss their name tags closest to the wall. Lisa always wanted to work the middle section, where you usually received better tips. Once a person works at Hooters, she may never want another job, because it is good, easy money.

Sometimes Lisa would work a double shift, which was 10:00 a.m. until midnight. The hours were long and hard but very much worth it most of the time. She misses Hooters and almost everyone who worked there. She was sad when she stopped working there.

After working at Hooters for a couple of years, Lisa met Duston Reed. It was almost like love at first sight. There was a certain connection the two of them shared that is unexplainable. He was a tall, dark, and very handsome member of the MOWA Band of the Choctaw Native American Tribe, with the most attractive smile she had ever seen. Lisa had her own apartment at this point, and once Duston became her boyfriend, he moved in with her right away. They were inseparable and had a great time together no matter what they were doing. Lisa thought their relationship was too good to be true and that she had finally found her bliss.

Duston Reed and Lisa Theris

The only problem was they were too much alike. They both were taking Xanax and Roxie pills, which they purchased off the streets. Roxicodone (known as "Roxys" or "Roxies") is a prescription semisynthetic opioid analgesic with highly addictive properties. This Schedule II narcotic is prescribed by doctors to immediately relieve moderate-to-severe chronic pain by affecting areas of the central nervous system of the body. Lisa had been continuously taking Xanax since she was a teenager. She felt she needed them to help with her anxiety. But Roxies were new to her and very addictive. Coming off those led to the worst withdrawals Lisa had ever had to go through.

Duston was a pipe fitter and had good jobs making very good money. Everyone who had ever worked with Duston would say he was a very hard worker when he actually applied himself.

Duston sometimes paid other Hooters girls to work Lisa's shifts so they could spend more time together. This would sometimes last up to a month at a time. Duston never kept the same job for very long because he constantly failed drug tests and skipped work. While he was in between jobs, he would spend the days at Hooters with Lisa while she was working. He was jealous and tried to keep a close eye on her.

Around this point, they began being abusive toward each other. They would yell and fuss, throw things, destroy each other's property (like cars and cell phones), and hit each other. Duston choked Lisa on a few occasions. Neighbors in the apartment complex would call the police when they heard the fights. It was very embarrassing for Lisa to go to work with bruises on her face. The customers would ask her what happened, and she would lie and tell them she had been in a car wreck. Lisa would have to get others to cover her shifts at work so she would not have to go and explain the bruises.

Four of Lisa's brothers met Duston and did not like him. They believed he was on drugs and was bad for Lisa. They knew he could not hold down a job and that he was a compulsive liar.

One night, Lisa was charged and convicted of domestic violence after she got intoxicated and pushed her sister while in the presence of a police officer. Her sister begged the officer to not press changes but the officer did anyway. Lisa's sister attended the court hearing with Lisa and explained that the situation was simply a misunderstanding. Nevertheless, the court required Lisa to attend anger management classes every Monday evening for an entire year. If she had skipped one class, she would have been sent to jail.

After living in Mobile and working at Hooters for almost four years, Lisa and her boyfriend, Duston, decided to move to Texas in July 2016. He was offered a great job opportunity with a pipe-fitting company.

Lisa Moves to Texas

• • •

LISA AND DUSTON MOVED TO Corpus Christi in July of 2016. Lisa left her apartment in Mobile, quit her job, and left her family to move to Texas. She was still in love with Duston and thought he had changed and that this could be a new beginning for them.

Her family knew Duston hit Lisa, and they were horrified at her decision to move with him so far away from where they could help her when she needed it. Some of her family stopped talking to her; they couldn't bear knowing what was going on and just pretending it was OK. It broke Lisa's heart that her family would not accept Duston, but she understood there point of view as to why they didn't approve of him. She hoped they would eventually accept him, but that time hasn't come yet.

Before they moved to Texas, Duston and Lisa would fight often, but Duston promised Lisa he would no longer hurt her if she would move to Texas with him. After moving to Texas, the abuse grew worse instead of better. Lisa had always fought back against Duston, but after moving to Texas, she grew afraid of him and stopped fighting back. Lisa was in Texas and did not know anyone. Duston did not allow her to work, and she would stay at the hotel and lay out by the pool most days.

Texas was not all bad. In the beginning, Lisa would get Duston's things ready for work, and she couldn't wait for him to return. She was proud of him for staying clean and being the man she needed him to be. He was working a night shift that began at 6:00 p.m. and ended at 6:00 a.m. the next day. While Duston slept for a few hours, Lisa would go swimming and work out in the hotel gym. She would always wake him up earlier than the time they had agreed upon so they could spend time together. They would go out to eat, go to the aquarium, or go to the mall. Lisa hated to shop, but Duston always insisted they go shopping and buy things for her. They also liked staying at the hotel and cuddling in the bed. It was like that for about the first two weeks.

Duston and Lisa could not find any Xanax while in Texas, so they began using heroin, which was the only drug they could find. Lisa would get sick and vomit each time she used heroin, but she would use it anyway because she was so depressed over her situation. Duston became hooked on heroin and would bring it to the hotel every day after work. Lisa tried to convince him to stop using heroin, but he wouldn't, so she kept using it along with him. Lisa could look into Duston's eyes and tell when he had been using drugs, and she realized he was addicted.

It is a terrible thing watching someone you love become addicted to heroin. It is unlike any other drug. The change you see in a person is not gradual, as is the case with many other drugs, but a change that can be seen almost immediately. Lisa wishes very much she had done things differently instead of going along with it. When she tried to hold her ground and demand Duston stop, he would only do it behind her back and lie about it.

He has a very big heart and loves hard, but he has dealt with a drug addiction from a young age. His drug addiction began as a result of losing his brother, who was his best friend. He starting using drugs to cope with that loss. His drug use progressively got worse and worse. Every time he begins doing well, he just goes right back to his old ways.

Duston made over $3,000 a week, but he still pawned Lisa's tablet twice to get more money for more drugs. After about two months, Lisa became more depressed with their lifestyle, and Duston didn't seem like the same person he once was, so she decided she wanted to move back home to Louisville, Alabama.

Duston would give money to Lisa daily, and she began saving some of the money so she could get home. She saved about $500 and packed all her belongings into her car to drive home so she could get out of the abusive relationship. She left the hotel en route to Alabama. First, she stopped to fill her car up with gas. After stopping, she looked in her hiding spot, which was under the lining of her jewelry box, and to her surprise, her money was gone. Lisa could not believe Duston had found her money under the lining in her jewelry box. Now she could not purchase gas or go anywhere, and the car was on empty. She was stranded at the gas station and didn't know the directions back to the hotel. She had no money to get home, and her phone was dead.

Three Hispanic men stopped near her car, and Lisa told them about her situation. They paid for her gas, and she decided to follow them back to their home to charge her phone and figure out what to do next. Two of them were nice and very respectful, but one was not. He told Lisa, "If you do something for me, I will help you get home."

Lisa told the other two men what he had said, and they said that was not the reason they were helping her and to ignore him. They went to a Spanish club. It was close to the main highway, and Lisa thought she could find her way back. After arriving at the hotel, Lisa asked Duston about her money. They argued about it for a while, and he finally convinced her to discuss it over dinner. When Lisa walked out of the hotel, her silver Chevrolet Malibu car had been repossessed—just that fast. Duston had recently purchased a new car and stopped making payments on Lisa's car, despite having promised to make her car payments if she agreed not to work.

Everything she owned was in that car. Duston had just bought a brand-new Mustang, and Lisa knew it would not be long before it too was repossessed or wrecked.

While Duston and Lisa had been in the process of purchasing the Mustang, the car salesman had driven them from his car lot to another car lot in his personal vehicle. While traveling there, Lisa noticed a hypodermic needle sticking in the back seat and asked the car salesman, "Did you know there was a needle stuck in this back seat?"

He said, "Oops, I must have thrown it out the window, and it blew back in." At that point, the car salesman and Duston began talking about heroin. Lisa believes Duston began purchasing heroin from the car salesman after that day.

Duston had told him what hotel they were staying at. The next day the car salesman unexpectedly showed up at the hotel where Lisa was staying, knowing that Duston would be at work. Lisa was surprised to see him. He asked her to go to church with him. She went with him because it gave her a chance to get out of the hotel for a few hours, and she was tired of being stuck there alone. They left the hotel and went to church that day. When Duston returned to the hotel, Lisa was not there. The girls at the front desk told him that Lisa had gone somewhere with a man. Duston called Lisa and told her the girls at the front desk had informed him of whom she was with.

When Lisa returned to the hotel, she was high on heroin. Lisa immediately proceeded to yell at the clerks at the hotel, and she fussed and cursed at them loudly for telling Duston she had left with another man.

Lisa acted so badly she was told to not return to the hotel, but she went to Duston's hotel room anyway. She and Duston got into a big fight. He began strangling her and she almost passed out. While Duston was strangling Lisa, she struck him on the head with something. She can't remember what she struck him with, but it was the first thing she could get her hands on. Later, after the fight, he said he had blacked out and did not remember hitting or strangling her. Duston told her that same story after each time he abused her.

Lisa put her bikini on and tried to leave the room and go down to the pool so she would not have to be around Duston and risk the chance of getting into another fight. While she was trying to leave the hotel room, Duston stopped her. They began to fight again. Lisa started screaming that Duston was trying to kill her. The ladies at the front desk heard Lisa screaming and called the police. When the police came, even though she had marks on her body from the beating, Lisa told the police he had not hit her, because she was afraid the police would lock him up and then he would lose his job. Lisa was almost arrested for public intoxication at that time. Duston helped talk the police out of locking her up. Lisa felt thankful that Duston had helped keep her from being locked up and decided to make up with him.

Things were still bad for Lisa and Duston. They would fuss and argue and then make up. She was never fully happy. Lisa hung out with the car salesman one more time. He tried to convince her to leave Duston and move in with him.

That night, Lisa and the car salesman had dinner with three of his friends. Duston called Lisa while she was having dinner, and she told him she was with the car salesman. Duston got mad, left work, and got fired. He began looking for them and kept calling Lisa's phone.

She was worried about Duston and asked the car salesman to take her back to the hotel to see him. She liked the man from the dealership, but only as a friend. She still loved Duston and didn't want their relationship to be ruined any more than it already was. He tried to persuade her to stay but finally took her back to the hotel. During the drive back to the hotel, the car salesman started yelling at Lisa. He stopped the vehicle and took out a new big-screen TV and smashed it on the ground to take out his anger.

He told Lisa he felt Duston would be waiting when they returned to the hotel, so they felt it would be best if he left her at a gas station. Duston went to the gas station and picked her up.

After that, Duston and Lisa decided to return to Alabama because they felt there was nothing left for them in Texas. Before leaving, Duston paid to get all her things out of her repossessed car. They barely had enough money to make it to Mobile. Before leaving Corpus Christi, they drove to a house that looked like a drug house.

A man walked up to the car, and they asked the man where they could find some Xanax, and he said he could get some next door. Duston gave him some money, and he went and purchased the Xanax and brought the pills back. Lisa took two Xanax, and Duston took five, and they began driving back to Alabama. After driving for about two hours, they almost crashed the vehicle.

Rain was falling heavily, and Duston was driving fast on an interstate. The car hit a puddle and spun around in a complete circle. The car scrubbed the guardrail alongside the highway.

Somehow, Duston managed to keep control of the car the whole time. Lisa thought she was going to die when the car was spinning around. She begged him to pull over and stop, but he convinced her that he could continue driving without wrecking.

On the way back to Alabama, Duston wanted to stop at a casino and gamble. Lisa kept telling Duston not to stop at the casino, because they would lose the little gas money they had. She knew Duston's worst problem, other than pills, was gambling. As with all people with a gambling addiction, he just didn't know when to stop. Duston kept telling her they were going to win. Duston put all the money on one bet, and he lost all of it, including their gas money. Lisa kept a one-dollar casino chip from that casino as a souvenir of being broke and having to beg people for money to get home so she would remember to never get in that situation again.

Duston stopped at a truck stop and tried to sell his expensive boots for gas money. A man whom Duston tried to sell the boots to refused to buy them, but he gave him money and told him to get Lisa home. He gave them his mailing address, and Duston promised to send him the money back when they got home. Duston claims to have lost the information, and Lisa regrets that, because she really wanted to pay him back.

They purchased gas, but it was not enough to get them home from Texas. Lisa could think of no other way to get more money for gas, and as a last resort, she called her parents and asked them to wire money to her to help get them home. Lisa was very ashamed to ask her parents for money, knowing how they felt about Duston and her decision to be with him in the first place.

Lisa and Duston finally arrived at Emanuel's home in Mobile, Alabama. Eman is Lisa's oldest brother. His wife and son were there also, and Lisa's father and mother were there visiting at the time. Lisa told Duston not to get out of the car because her family did not like him, but he insisted on helping Lisa carry her belongings to the house. Lisa could not believe Duston got out of the car.

Lisa's dad and brother stayed in the house so there would be no confrontation. Duston left, and Lisa rode home with her parents to Louisville, Alabama. She slept the whole way.

Lisa Returns to Louisville, Alabama

• • •

AFTER RETURNING TO LOUISVILLE, LISA was trying to figure out what she wanted to do next in her life. At this point, Lisa stopped using drugs. She stayed home for several months, recovering from her drug addiction and the inevitable withdrawals. She was depressed, and it was a very, very dark time in her life. She would go see her brothers Will and Rob some weekends in Mobile, just to get away. That was the only time she would leave her home in Louisville. Lisa did not let her friends in the Louisville area know she was back home, because she wanted to be alone.

Rob, Lisa, Lizzy and Will Theris

Lisa, along with her mom and dad, made a plan. She would go back to school to be a radiology technician. Lisa was trying to straighten her life out, but she was very depressed. She started going to doctors and was diagnosed with bipolar disorder.

Lisa's doctor prescribed medicine to help her with depression and anxiety. She tried several different antidepressants, but none seemed to help. One of the bipolar medicines made her gain twenty pounds in three weeks. Lisa did not want to gain weight, and she stopped taking the medicine. Her doctor tried many different bipolar medications, but they all made her gain weight, so she did not take any of them.

Lisa began attending Wallace Community College (Wallace) in Eufaula, Alabama, in January of 2017. She was doing really well in school during her first semester at Wallace. She was drug-free, attended all classes, and was making good grades through the end of the semester in May of 2017.

The Weeks Leading Up to
Lisa's Disappearance

• • •

LISA BEGINS GOING DOWN THE WRONG PATH

IN JUNE OF 2017, LISA began her second semester at Wallace. At that point, Lisa started hanging out with an old friend, Ronald, with whom she had worked at the Piggly Wiggly grocery store in Brundidge, Alabama, and with whom she had attended school in Ariton, Alabama. They had fun spending time together. They did things together like going arrowhead hunting, going on nature adventures, and just goofing off. He introduced her to some people, those people introduced her to other people, and that is when she fell in with the wrong crowd.

Lisa and Ronald would hang out at a spot in Ariton, Alabama. The hangout was a house they would go to and use a drug called "ice." Lisa thought this was weird. Everyone used to smoke weed and drink alcohol several years earlier at the time she had left Louisville; now everyone was doing ice. Ice is the purest and most potent form of methamphetamine. It comes in the form of shards that look like ice and is usually snorted, injected, or smoked. Lisa preferred snorting ice because she felt smoking it would rot her teeth. She wasn't aware that ice was a form of crystal meth until she had been using it for a few months.

Lisa met a young lady named Desiree who lived in Troy, Alabama, around May 2017. Lisa and Desiree immediately became good friends and were practically inseparable. Through Desiree, she met Richard John Jefferson (Richard), and through Richard she met George Lee Harvey (Lee), who also lived in Troy. Lisa said Richard was really nice to her, but they never had a sexual relationship. Richard was married.

As Lisa began snorting ice more often, she began staying awake for days at a time.

Lisa said she was never really addicted to ice. She liked downers, not uppers, and tried ice because everyone else was doing it. When she lived in Louisville before moving away, it was easy to get pills, which is what she liked, but being back in Louisville now, all she could get was ice.

Lisa would not go home for many days at a time. She would attend classes at Wallace in the daytime and would stay at different friends' homes at night.

She never had been one to sleep around, although in the drug circle, people did switch partners quite often, and everyone dated everyone. That is one part of the drug world that she managed not to be a part of. Friends called it "the Circle," because everyone would just keep switching up and going back to one another. When Lisa would finally get home after being gone for days, all she wanted to do was sleep. It was totally unlike Lisa to stay gone, because her parents were like her best friends. She loved spending time with them.

Lisa was quickly changing, but she could not see it. She was not the same fun-loving daughter, sister, or friend who her loved ones once knew. Lisa could not imagine the pain and stress that she was putting her parents through. The people she was hanging out with became like a new family to her. She would spend almost all her time hanging out with them, using ice, and staying up for days at a time.

Lisa Arrested in Coffee County, Alabama

Lisa was charged with disorderly conduct in Elba, Alabama, in the summer of 2017. She had gone to court with a friend's mom, Donna, whose son was on trial for domestic violence. Lisa was close friends with Donna's son and wanted to be there with her for support. When court was over, she walked outside.

Lisa noticed a deputy walking closely behind her. The deputy told Donna to give up her grandchild or go to jail. Lisa and Donna were scared. Lisa expressed her opinion to the deputy, and she told him, "If something happens to that child, you are going to feel bad." The deputy grabbed Lisa's arm. She told him he was hurting her.

The deputy put Lisa in handcuffs, told her she was being charged with disorderly conduct, and took her to jail. She stayed in jail for about three hours and then was released on a bond after paying $145. Charges were dropped a few months later while Lisa was lost in the woods.

Lisa in Serious Car Wreck Nine Days before Getting Lost

Lisa and another woman from Pike County were in a car wreck in Georgia on July 9, 2017, just after making a drug deal. Lisa said it was a terrible car accident.

Lisa was traveling on a four-lane highway and was in the left lane passing a car in the right lane. The person in the right lane was texting and crossed over into Lisa's lane, and Lisa had to swerve in order to try to avoid a collision. Lisa lost control of her vehicle; it rolled and ended up in the woods. All the windows in the vehicle were shattered, and the top of the vehicle on the driver's side was bent down. Lisa had really liked that little car. It was a Toyota Matrix, and it was now completely totaled.

Lisa and the other person were taken to the emergency room by ambulance. Lisa had a horrible headache, but she did not want treatment because the girl who was in an accident with her was acting obnoxious. She was loud and disruptive and was complaining about everything, and Lisa just wanted to get away from her. Weeks later an MRI scan would reveal bulging disks in Lisa's neck and lower back. Two of Lisa's friends drove to the hospital to pick up her and the other person and then drove them home.

Hunting Lodge Allegedly Burglarized; Lisa Enters the Woods

• • •

LISA RODE WITH Richard John Jefferson to a location very near a hunting lodge in Midway, Alabama, on July 18, 2017. It was there that Lisa says she saw Richard John Jefferson and George Lee Harvey break into and enter the hunting lodge that day. Lisa believed that Richard and Lee were going to harm her because they thought she was going to report them to law enforcement, so Lisa went deeper into the woods and soon became lost. She spent the next twenty-five days in the woods.

On July 17, 2017, the day before the supposed burglary, Richard had called Lisa's friend Ronald around 4:00 p.m. and asked to speak with Lisa. Richard told Lisa that he needed her help with something. She said OK. Her guess was the ride had something to do with drugs. She did not ask any questions. Lisa said Ronald told her a million times not to go anywhere with Richard. She later knew she should have listened.

Richard had always been respectful and nice to Lisa, and she trusted him. Richard drove to Ronald's house late that afternoon and picked her up, and they drove to Lee's house. Richard had helped get Lee bonded out of jail earlier that day.

This was the first day that Lisa met Lee. He seemed like a normal, nice guy, but she never really got to know him very well, and they were not friends.

Two other men were also at Lee's house when they arrived. They all hung out together for a while. Later that evening Lisa and Richard went arrowhead hunting using flashlights. They stayed out all night long, riding around. They planned for Lisa, Lee, and Richard to meet up again at six the next morning.

The morning of July 18, 2017, the day of the supposed burglary, as soon as the sun began to rise, Lisa and Richard went to a pond and played with binoculars.

Lisa and Richard met at Lee's house around 6:00 a.m. Lee was still at home asleep, but he woke up and let them come inside. Lee was not ready to go yet, because someone was using his pickup truck. Lisa, Richard, and Lee remained at his house until about 10:00 a.m., when Lee's friend returned his truck. Richard and Lisa left Lee's around 11:00 a.m., heading to Midway, Alabama. They rode in a red pickup truck pulling a trailer. She did not know where they were going or why he wanted her to go and wasn't concerned enough to ask.

They rode to Midway, and when they arrived, Richard told her the reason he needed her assistance. He said they were going to burglarize a hunting lodge. He told Lisa the hunting lodge belonged to Lee's father. He also told her the insurance company would pay for the property that was stolen. He made her believe they weren't doing anything wrong because the owners had told him to do it.

Upon arriving in Midway, they began looking for a gas station. They were told it was many miles to the nearest gas station, so they went to Dollar General in Midway and purchased rubbing alcohol to pour in the gas tank so they could make it to the hunting camp. Richard told Lisa to call Lee and tell him to bring them some gas for his truck.

After leaving Dollar General, they proceeded down Bullock County Road 47 and backed the truck and trailer into a driveway across the road from the hunting camp. After Richard backed the truck up, they sat for hours, waiting on Lee. Since Lisa's cell phone had been stolen nine days earlier while she was in the hospital emergency room, she used Richard's phone to log in to her Facebook page. She spent a lot of time playing with binoculars while waiting for Lee to arrive.

They were parked, partially hidden in the woods. Richard was backed into a driveway that led into the woods. They probably could have been seen from the road if someone driving down Bullock County Road 47 had looked up the driveway. Lisa noticed Richard was looking and acting much differently from normal, as if drugs were changing his character. Lisa knew he had had no sleep for several days.

Lee finally arrived around 3:30 p.m. He was driving a tiny old pickup truck. It was a dingy dark-red color and looked like it had been painted with spray paint. Richard was still backed in and facing the highway. Lee pulled in forward, and the vehicles were facing each other, bumper to bumper. Lee got out and came to Richard's truck, and they talked. Lee and Richard put gas in Richard's truck. Next, they all got into Lee's truck, and Lee showed Richard and Lisa the gate to use to access the hunting lodge.

As they approached the hunting lodge, they stopped just before the wooden bridge. The bridge was pretty long, and there was no top over it. It goes over the pond to get to the property. While stopped, Richard and Lee sniffed ice. They then proceeded across the bridge to get to the hunting lodge. Lisa heard Richard and Lee talking about the cameras; Lee told Richard he had taken care of most of them.

Then they all rode back to Richard's truck, where Lisa told them she didn't want to go back to the hunting lodge. Lisa thinks Lee went up the road to be on look out. He was supposed to call if he heard police sirens or if somebody came looking or riding down the road. Lisa didn't want to go back to the hunting lodge with Richard, but she did.

Richard and Lisa went back across the wooden bridge in Richard's truck this time. Richard had left the trailer they had towed to the property at the spot where they were parked. After crossing the bridge, Richard began beating on a doorknob on a side door, trying to break into the building. Lisa told Richard she wanted to leave and went and sat in his truck. She said over and over, "I am not doing this." He told Lisa that he was already there, and he was going to do it. Lisa got fed up and ran to a wooded area near the wooden bridge and took her shoes off because she didn't want Richard to be able to find her. Her shoes were neon orange, and she thought they were bright enough to be seen. She began making her way back to the road they had come from. Lisa could hear Richard banging loudly on the door and decided to go back to him one more time and ask him to leave. She told him they both needed to leave. She told him if they didn't leave, he would go to jail for doing this. She told him what he was doing was stupid, pointing out that he couldn't even get in the door.

At that point he told Lisa to get in his truck. She did and thought they were about to leave, but instead Richard rammed the garage door of the building with his truck and drove partially into the building.

He must not have cared if his truck got damaged. The roll-up garage door opened just a little less than halfway. Lisa told Richard to take her somewhere so she could sit and wait on them. She insisted that she was not going to be involved with the alleged burglary. Lisa thought they were good friends, and she was begging, pleading, and trying to get him to leave.

Richard seemed upset that Lisa would not assist him in the suspected burglary, but he agreed to take her back near the highway and dropped her off on the south side of County Road 47. Lisa got out of the truck and sat in the woods, staying there for a little while before deciding to go wait by the trailer. If the cops came, she did not want to be near the hunting lodge. Lisa could not see Richard or Lee from her location. She walked back to the trailer. She believes Richard was in his truck getting more stuff from the hunting camp. Lisa never saw Lee go with Richard, but she thinks he was trailing him back and forth.

She knew that Richard was angry with her for not helping with the alleged burglary, and she was scared. She did not want to be at the trailer in case law enforcement drove up, but she wanted to be close enough to get back to the truck when it was time to leave. This is the point when Lisa began her twenty-five days lost in the woods.

Hunting Lodge Alleged Burglary Reported to Bullock County Sheriff's Department

• • •

THE HUNTING CAMP HAD SURVEILLANCE cameras and an alarm system. The owner of the lodge, who resided in Florida, was notified by the alarm system that the hunting camp had been broken into and was able to review the surveillance video remotely from Florida. The owner reported the suspected burglary to the Bullock County Sheriff's Department. After further investigation, surveillance video and other evidence led them to believe Richard and Lee had supposedly burglarized the hunting camp.

Arrest warrants were issued for Richard John Jefferson and George Lee Harvey. Law enforcement said the suspected theft involved four-wheelers, ATVs, tools, chainsaws, and other items valued at approximately $40,000.

Lisa Reported Missing

• • •

Lisa Joy Theris was reported missing to the Troy Police Department on July 23, 2017, by her father and two of her friends. According to her father, his last contact with Lisa was by phone on Tuesday, July 18, 2017. During that phone conversation, Lisa told her father she was in Troy, Alabama. Lisa's father said a lot of people had been looking for her. He also said he talked to her every day or every other day, and it was absolutely unlike Lisa to not contact them for this length of time.

The Troy Police Department began to investigate Lisa's disappearance. At this point, law enforcement concentrated in the Troy, Alabama, area because she had told her father she was in Troy during their last phone conversation. Troy Police Department had very few leads to follow in the beginning.

Soon after Lisa was reported missing, Richard gave law enforcement a tip that Lisa was actually last seen near a hunting camp in Midway, Alabama, at the time it was allegedly burglarized and either fled into the woods or left in a vehicle.

At that point, the Bullock County Sheriff's Department became involved in the search. Bullock County Sheriff Raymond

Rodgers, Bullock County Chief Deputy Anthony Williams, and Bullock County Deputy Sheriff Chad Faulkner began working on the suspected burglary case and the case of Lisa's disappearance. It was then believed by law enforcement the two cases were possibly connected.

Jefferson and Harvey Arrested

• • •

RICHARD JOHN JEFFERSON, AGE THIRTY-ONE, was arrested on Monday, July 31, 2017, and charged with burglary in the third degree and theft in the first degree for the burglary and theft at the hunting camp in Midway, Alabama.

A deputy sheriff with the Pike County Sheriff Department spotted Richard driving a white Cadillac on Alabama Highway 87 near the Pike County Lake Road just outside the Troy, Alabama, city limits. The deputy was aware of the existing warrants for Richard and turned around to make contact with him. Richard was traveling toward Troy and fled from the officer in his vehicle and later on foot. Officers searched an area and located him in the back seat of a car in the 600 block of Wilson Drive in Troy. His vehicle was found nearby on Rick Street and impounded, and he was transported to the Bullock County Jail.

George Lee Harvey, age thirty-six, was arrested on Friday, August 4, 2017, and charged with burglary in the third degree and theft in the first degree for the July 18 incident at the hunting camp in Midway, Alabama.

Troy police officers attempted to stop a black 2009 Chevrolet Tahoe driven by Lee at approximately 11:00 p.m. on August 4, 2017, on Pike County Road 1177 just outside the Troy city limits.

Lee fled from the officers and led them on a pursuit through Pike, Montgomery, and Crenshaw Counties until the vehicle ran out of gas. Lee then fled on foot into the woods, where officers found him and took him into custody on existing warrants as well as additional charges of attempting to elude a police officer, driving with a suspended license, failure to signal, and reckless driving. He was placed in the Pike County Jail. Richard and Lee were placed in separate jails to prevent them from communicating with each other.

Richard's and Lee's bonds were each set at $250,000. Richard had no prior felonies, while Lee had served time for drugs and bad checks.

Richard and Lee were both questioned extensively by law-enforcement officials about Lisa's disappearance, but the questioning did not lead authorities to Lisa. In fact, some of the answers given may have misled law enforcement and hindered the search.

Law-Enforcement Search

• • •

AFTER LISA'S DISAPPEARANCE WAS REPORTED on July 23, 2017, the Troy Police Department opened an investigation that was later turned over to the Bullock County Sheriff's Department. It was believed Lisa was last seen at the hunting camp and either fled into the woods near the hunting camp or left the area in a vehicle. At that point, the Bullock County Sheriff's Department took the lead in the investigation, since it was believed Lisa was last seen in Bullock County.

After further investigation by the Bullock County Sheriff's Department, leads and tips led to a search for Lisa in Bullock County near the hunting lodge on August 2, 2017. The area searched was on the south side of Bullock County Road 47 in Midway, Alabama.

The search parties used cadaver dogs and believed they were searching for a dead body. Lisa's father took some of her clothing from home to the search party. He was not aware that the dogs were cadaver dogs. Lisa's clothes were used to familiarize the dogs with her scent. A large number of law-enforcement agencies assisted in the search, including Bullock County Sheriff's Department; Alabama Department of Conservation; Easterling Correctional Facility; Troy Police Department; Clayton Police Department;

Pike County Sheriff's Dive Team; Ventress Correctional Facility; K-9 Specialty from Columbiana, Alabama; Tallaco K-9 from Dadeville, Alabama; and employees from the State of Alabama Lands Division. Bullock County Deputy Sheriff Chad Faulkner and Conservation Officer Bill Freeman helped organize the search.

Search team who looked for Lisa Theris while she was lost

This search did not produce any leads about Lisa's whereabouts, as she was actually lost in the woods on the north side of Bullock County Road 47 during the time of the search. The search parties did not search on the north side of County Road 47 because all their tips and investigations had led them to believe she was on the south side of the road. The areas searched were vast. Thousands of acres of rural forest are located in that portion of Bullock County.

The searchers used ATVs, trucks, and boats while searching for Lisa. A dive team searched portions of a pond. The large search party spent an entire day in the area. On other days, Bullock County law enforcement searched many other areas, including under bridges, near rivers and streams, and other various wooded areas in Bullock County. They reviewed surveillance videos and followed every lead and tip.

Bullock County Sheriff's Department dedicated many days and work hours in search of Lisa. They never stopped searching, even though many people who gave them tips claimed she was dead.

Lisa's Father Searches for His Baby

• • •

Soon after Lisa was reported missing, Lisa's father, William Theris, went to Richard Jefferson's house to question him about Lisa's disappearance. Lisa's friend Myisha went with him. Richard said for them to meet at the movie theater in Troy, and he would go show them where to look for Lisa. William and Myisha went to the movie theater and waited on Richard, but he never showed up. They repeatedly called and texted Richard, but he didn't reply.

Next, Myisha was able to find out where Lee's home was located. Lisa's father and Myisha went to his home, and as they suspected, Richard's truck was there. Lisa's father knocked on the door and on the windows, but no one came out. He kept yelling that he wanted to find his daughter, but nobody came out of the house. William pretended to leave but just hid his car a short distance away and walked back to the house. Richard then came out of Lee's trailer. Lisa's father demanded Richard tell him where his daughter was, and Richard told him to ask a longtime friend of Lisa's, Maxine, and she would tell him. Lisa's father later contacted Maxine, and she told him she didn't know where Lisa was located and didn't know why Richard had told him that.

Lisa Theris and her father, William Theris

Lisa Survives Twenty-Five Days in the Woods

• • •

The First Few Days in the Woods

Lisa entered the woods on July 18, 2017, around dusk with no clothes, no food, no phone—absolutely nothing except the will to survive.

When Richard and Lee had completed the yet unproven burglary and were getting ready to leave the area, Lisa was still hiding in the woods and overheard Richard and Lee talking.

Something they said led her to believe they were going to kill her. Therefore, she crawled away, trying to hide from them, and took off her bright-red shirt because it could be easily seen. She hid in a gully or low area in the woods and hoped they would not find her. She hid because she felt at this point if she ran, they would see her.

While in the gully, she closed her eyes and began praying they would not find her. She heard Richard and Lee walking in her direction. As they got close, she felt the only way to survive was to play dead.

At this point, either from exhaustion, being extremely scared, or being drugged, Lisa passed out. She had been awake for more than thirty-six hours.

After that, her memory gets blurry for a while. Lisa learned from Dr. Smolinski that her memory has likely become blurry from this traumatic experience. Part of a person's brain can keep certain things that happen away from other parts of the brain. This is a natural way for humans to protect the mind from severe psychological issues.

Next, she remembers seeing Lee walking away from her, but she is not sure if that was the same day or the next day.

She later remembers waking up at nighttime in a dome or a bowl-shaped area. She couldn't move and could barely open her eyes, and even today, she doesn't know why. She heard Maxine telling someone to "shoot her up." Lisa believes she was being repeatedly drugged so that men could have sex with her. She specifically remembers one man saying, "I don't want her until she is all the way dead."

After that night, the next thing she remembers is waking up during the daytime, deep in the woods, totally naked. This was probably a day or two after she initially entered the woods. She doesn't know what happened to the rest of her clothes, other than the shirt she took off to remain hidden. Her clothes have never been found. When Lisa entered the woods, she had on a brightly colored shirt, khaki shorts, bra, and panties.

Waking up in the woods naked with none of her belongings was the most awful thing that has happened to Lisa in her entire life. But not remembering how she even got there was incredibly scary. Not only did she not know where she was or how she got there but she also could not clearly remember what had happened the previous days. She was very scared and confused.

Lisa believes it is likely that someone tried to overdose her during the first few days she was lost in the woods. She has a big scar in the middle of her left arm where her vein is. It looks like someone stuck a needle in her arm many times. She doesn't know what kind of drug the person used, but it was possibly heroin.

Her contact lenses were no longer in her eyes, and she is legally blind without her contacts or glasses. She can see without them, but her vision is very blurry. She was diagnosed as being legally blind when she was about ten years old. Lisa heard one of her supposed friends, Maxine, along with Habitha, who was Maxine's girlfriend, talking to Bent. They said his name was Bent Elroy; Lisa said she had never met him before or after being lost in the woods, but she later found out his name matches up to a real person who is friends with Maxine and Habitha and is an ice drug dealer.

Lisa was begging them for water, food, and clothes. Lisa thought it was a messed-up prank in the beginning. She told them her parents would give them money to get her home. They once told her they would take her home, but they never did.

Maxine, Habitha, and Bent came a second time sometime during her first few days in the woods. Lisa again begged them for water, food, and clothes.

Maxine told Lisa she didn't have any extra clothes and would go to the store, purchase food and water, and bring it back to her. As they were leaving, Maxine said, "Get it over with, and put her in a river." After that time, when they left, Lisa went very far away from that location, because they obviously weren't going to help her, and Lisa thought they would eventually kill her.

Lisa is not sure whether some of what she remembers truly happened or whether she was hallucinating. In addition to feeling like she had been drugged, Lisa did not eat or drink anything during the first three days.

AFTER THE FIRST FEW DAYS

Lisa thought no one was looking for her. While in the woods, Lisa once heard a helicopter. She wondered if it was looking for her, but she never saw it.

She did not see any animals, but one night she did hear an animal coming toward her head while she was lying on the ground. She thought it may be a possum or skunk but was too scared to look. She lay very still for a while and finally looked, and it was gone.

Rain fell heavily for many days while Lisa was in the woods. During the heavy rains, she placed big leaves or branches on top of her naked body to try not to get wet when it rained, but that never worked.

Once, Lisa heard stomping and something running; it sounded like two feet were coming toward her. She thought, *Should I try to run or stay still?* Lisa thought it might be a person who could help, and she screamed out, "Hey!" but nobody answered. Whatever it was just walked away.

She was always on the move, looking for food, water, shelter, or a way out—except during the nighttime. Nights were the absolute worst times.

Lisa tried to keep track of how long she was lost by counting nights and days. She would try to keep up with it in her mind.

Red bug bites covered her entire body. The bugs were extremely horrible at night, swarming and crawling all over her body all night long. Unable to sleep, Lisa would slap and swat at the bugs for hours.

At times Lisa was so scared she would scream out her family member's names. Lisa would start with her mom and then go to her dad and call out her brothers' and sisters' names. She would yell each of their names: Mom, Dad, Lizzy, Rob, Will, Angie, Becky, Johnny, Chris, Nate, Eman, Guillaume, Johnny, Nick, Marianne, and Mike. She has two brothers named Johnny. She would scream loud. She would scream and scream. She would scream "Help!" for hours. But she called out for her mom the most. She would talk out loud and hope that her family could hear her. It was unthinkable to her that she could be screaming so loudly and still no one heard her.

Lisa was the most scared during the nighttime hours. Being alone and naked in total darkness was almost unbearable. Because of fear, she did not usually sleep any during the nighttime. She would find a large tree with roots that came out from the base and lie down in between the roots as close to the tree as possible. For some reason, being close to a large tree brought her a little comfort. She would often break thin, leafy branches from trees and use them to cover her body at night to help stay warm.

Some nights, the moon dimly lit the area. As soon as the sun rose in the morning, Lisa would sleep for several hours. This was the only time she could sleep somewhat in peace.

Lisa remembers a scary nightmare that she had one night while in the woods. The dream seemed so real and vivid to Lisa. It was pitch-black dark. Lisa could not see anything and lay on the ground next to a tree being bitten by insects. She could feel every single bite. It seemed worse than most nights. She could feel them tearing into her flesh everywhere on her bare-naked body. The pain was so intolerable, she was screaming and yelling like she never had yelled before. "Make it stop!" she would scream. Suddenly she heard rustling in the leaves. "Help! You are here to save me, aren't you?" Lisa asked. Out of nowhere, three figures were suddenly right upon her. They looked like aliens, but all three were different shape and sizes. One was very tall and had no eyes that she could see, one was normal in height with the shape of some sort of dinosaur head, and the other was very short and had big bulging eyes. The small one and the one with the dinosaur head did most of the talking. They told her they could take her away from all the pain, and if she did not give in, there would be much more suffering coming her way. They told her that her death would be slow and painful and the coyotes would eat her body so she would never be found. They said her parents' hearts would never be put at ease. She said nothing; she just stared up at the creatures in shock.

Finally, the tall one with no eyes said to them, "Let us go now to the others."

Then a voice that could not actually be heard aloud and belonged to no one who could be seen said to Lisa, "You have been strong, but now it is time to let go. I have been waiting for you."

She said to the voice, "You may take my body, but you will never have my soul."

The voice laughed at her and replied, "I have taken your body many years ago." Lisa began rolling around on the ground and making strange sounds she had never made before. This went on for what seemed like hours. In her mind she prayed for this evil to stay away from her. She prayed and prayed. Lisa finally woke up. It was still totally dark, but morning was near. She could hear coyotes howling in the distance but somehow felt safe.

Each day, after sleeping for several hours, she would spend the rest of the day walking and searching for food, water, and a way out. This became a routine for many days.

She found what appeared to be fresh, clean water in what she later found out was named the South Fork Cowikee Creek. The creek was about fifteen feet wide, and the banks of the creek were about ten feet high and very steep to climb up and down. The volume of water flowing in the base of the creek varied depending on the amount of rainfall. While Lisa was there, the flow of the water was a few feet wide and about one inch deep. Lisa calls the creek "Sand Bar Creek" because the creek bed was sandy. She drank water from that creek almost every day. The water was cold and crystal clear.

She was often afraid to venture very far from the creek, because that was the only good, clean drinking water she had located, and she was scared she would not be able to find her way back to the creek if she went too far from it. Several times Lisa had traveled too far from the creek, and she'd had no water for two days at a time.

Lisa had no idea which direction she should travel to find her way out. When walking away from the creek, she didn't know if she was going deeper into the woods or getting closer to finding her way out.

While in the woods, Lisa ate muscadines, mushrooms, and a few snails. She tried to eat leaves, but they tasted terrible, and she couldn't force herself to swallow them. She would eat up to about four mushrooms and twelve muscadines on the days she could find them. Some days she wasn't able to find any and would eat nothing for the entire day.

Muscadines are similar to grapes, except they grow in clusters of four or more fruits rather than in tight bunches. They are about one inch to one and a half inches in diameter. The muscadines were the best-tasting food Lisa ate. They were delicious. But it was often difficult to find ripe ones. She would spit the seeds out.

Lisa knew some mushrooms were poisonous to eat, but she felt eating them was better than dying from starvation. Lisa would not eat the big, bright mushrooms, because she had a sense they were poisonous. The snails were tiny, about the size of the tip of her pinky finger. They tasted like dirt. She was unable to locate any other food to eat.

During the time Lisa was in the woods, her arms and legs were usually numb. She discovered shortly after being found that she had bulging disks in her lower back and neck, which she believes were caused from a car accident nine days before becoming lost in the woods. The bulging disks were causing the numbness.

Due to the numbness, she would often crawl on her hands and knees. She eventually found a small bush. She uprooted it and snapped the branches off until it was in the shape of a walking cane and she could use it as a walking stick.

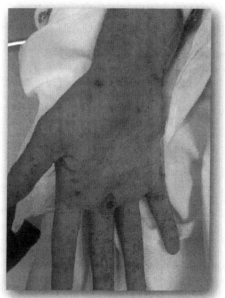

Splinters, cut and scratches can been seen on Lisa Theris' hand.

Not being able to brush her teeth was very unpleasant. She would use small twigs to scrub her teeth clean. She often had thoughts of how wonderful it would be just to brush her teeth and take a warm bath.

Lisa was supposed to have a menstrual cycle during the time she was lost, but she did not have one, probably because of the extreme stress placed upon her body due to the lack of food and water, as well as being lost.

Lisa's Christian faith helped her maintain a somewhat positive spirit. She talked to God very often while she was in the woods. She felt like He was with her the entire time.

The first time it rained heavily while she was in the woods, she located a big tree that was uprooted, and there was room for her to lie underneath and be sheltered. Lisa remembers another time it rained for what felt like two days straight. She was not near the big tree that was uprooted, but she located another tree that was leaning over, and she lay underneath it. The tree was just wide enough to keep her from getting too wet. If she stuck her legs up and put her feet on the tree or lay on her stomach flat on the ground, she felt dryer. She said after spending about twelve days in the woods, she started to lose her mind.

Once, she was near the sandbar and thought she saw her father walk up and say, "Come on, silly goose; it is wet out here." She imagined he took her hand and led her out of the woods. Then Lisa imagined she saw the two of them leaving the woods. Sometimes she would close her eyes and begin to imagine herself being at home.

Another time she imagined her sister Lizzy came to her and said, "Your soul is leaving, but your body is still attached to the woods. It is time for you to let go." Lisa tried hard to let go, but something would not let her. Lisa believes that if she had managed to let go all the way, she would have died.

One day, Lisa felt a huge bubble on her ear. At first, she didn't know if she should pull it off or not, but she did. It looked like a huge, soft sack with no eyes, no legs, and no mouth. She burst it open, and it was full of blood. Lisa said for a split-second she thought of drinking it. She was just that thirsty. Not too long after pulling the bug off her ear, she pulled another one from her eyelid. These things were huge and had been feasting on Lisa. She later learned they were ticks.

She occasionally drank water from mud puddles when she had journeyed too far from the Sand Bar Creek. After drinking from the mud puddles, she would often lay her naked body in the puddle to help cool off during the summer heat. She would always drink before lying in the puddle because her body was so dirty. Once, she was in a muddy area and began to sink into the ground. She thought it was quicksand and became very scared. She quickly left the area where the soft mud was located.

Every night Lisa would try to find a tree when it started to get dark. There was something soothing about trees that made her feel safer. She thought it was funny that she needed to get to a tree before dark. It wasn't just a wooded area she was lost in; there were many large fields too.

There was little sleep to be had for Lisa; she guesses that she averaged about three hours per twenty-four-hour period. At night the bugs would come and swarm on her. If she picked the wrong spot to try to sleep, the swarms would be especially bad. The bugs were attacking her, and all she could do was swat, swat, swat.

The Last Few Days

As Lisa neared the end of her dreadful stay in the woods, her body had become frail and weak. She had open wounds on the bottoms of her feet and on her legs, as well as many thorns and stickers. Each step was painful. She was having a difficult time maintaining hope of survival. She had gone from 154 pounds down to 107 pounds. Mentally she had become very unstable and was beginning to think her life was about to come to an end. Her will to survive kept her moving.

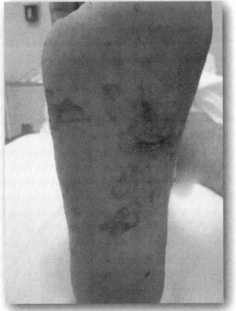

The bottom of Lisa Theris' foot
just after being found.

Two days before being found, she came across a deer-hunting stand. It was old, but it looked like someone had recently rebuilt the steps. The steps going up to the top of the stand were very steep, and her weak body could barely climb them. She was praying that she would find water stored there for a hunter or just anything left behind that she could use. When she opened the door on the stand, the only thing inside were two very old chairs. One had a cushion, and it was extremely dirty. She hated to sit her naked body on it, but it had been so long since she had sat on anything but the ground. She sat on it, and it felt so good that she nodded off to sleep. When she awoke, she decided she should get down, for fear of her weight making the deer stand topple over. *Oh no*, she thought, *these terrible steps again.* She slowly made her way down. Once she reached the ground, she was so tired that she lay down on the ground beside the deer stand. The blazing sun was now pounding down on Lisa.

When she turned and looked at the ground, she saw a tooth and more teeth crushed into pieces beside it. She wondered how the teeth got there. She wanted to take them with her but had nothing to carry them in.

She got up and started toward the wooded area again. It had started pouring down rain. Lisa tried to catch the rain in her mouth and was surprised when this did not work. She then tried using leaves to catch the rain. The leaves worked better, but it took too much time to get a good amount of water to drink. Finally, after being drenched in rain, she had the idea of wringing the water out of her long hair and drinking it. She knew it was disgusting, but she was thirsty, and it was water.

Although she was thankful for the rain, it seemed to be raining for hours, and she did not travel in the rain. She started praying silently to God to please let the sun come out. Then she started talking out loud to God to please let the sun come out. Slowly the clouds moved out of the sun's way. Then she started singing praises to God. She made up the following song:

Let the sun shine, shine on me.
Let the sun shine, shine on me.
I can feel your love, your love,
Shining down on me.
Shining down on me.

I'm feeling your love, your love,
Shining right down on me.
Let me feel it, I can feel it,
Your warming love, saving me,
Your love saving me.

Lisa kept singing this song, and the sun came out. The sun was right over her. It was still raining around her, but she couldn't feel the rain. All she felt was warmth.

Weather records show rainfall was recorded on eleven days, and the total amount of rainfall was 7.12 inches during the time Lisa was lost in the woods. The maximum temperature was ninety-eight degrees, and the minimum temperature was sixty-two degrees.

On Lisa's final day in the woods, she finally made it close enough to a road where she could hear traffic. She told herself, *Today is the day.* She had to get out. She thought, *I have to make it.* To begin with, it was difficult to tell the exact direction of the sounds of the traffic. She went in several different directions but finally made her way to a clear-cut path. The sound of the traffic became louder and louder. She knew she was getting closer.

As she worked her weak, almost lifeless body closer to the road, she used her walking stick to fight her way through briars. The briars were sticking in her legs and feet, but she continued, because she knew the roadway was near. Lisa thought, *Finally, a miracle!* She saw a road and cars passing by. But there was one more obstacle: the roadway had an extremely steep bank. She worked her way to the top on her hands and knees. As she neared the edge of the roadway, the extreme heat, sun, and exhaustion caused her to collapse. She lay there for a short period of time, hoping someone would see her lying only a few feet from the roadway.

She was still afraid, for she had no idea who would find her. Would this person help her or harm her? Several cars and trucks passed, but no one saw her. She finally made one last effort to raise her arm as a car was drawing near. The driver of that car noticed Lisa and turned around. Lisa's nightmare was over.

Lisa Found and Taken to the Emergency Room

• • •

Judy Garner Spots Lisa beside the Highway

While traveling east on Highway 82 near Midway, Alabama, Judy Garner spotted a naked girl on the side of the road. At first glance Judy thought the girl was a deer. She turned her vehicle around, stopped in the highway, and quickly walked toward the girl. She had found Lisa Joy Theris, who had been missing for twenty-five days.

Lisa said, "Help me," and then laid her head back on the ground. Garner called 911, and Bullock County Sheriff Raymond Rodgers and Bullock County Deputy Sheriff Anthony Williams responded to the call. While waiting on law enforcement to arrive, Judy gave Lisa a pair of men's boxer shorts and a man's purple button-up shirt and helped dress her. She also gave Lisa a Boost drink and a bottle of Dasani water. The driver of a FedEx truck also stopped to help. The driver allowed Lisa to sit in the air-conditioned FedEx truck so she could cool off. Judy stayed with Lisa until law enforcement arrived.

Judy Gardner and Lisa Theris

Deputy Williams transported Lisa to the Bullock County Hospital in the back seat of his car. Lisa's first drink after arriving at Bullock County Hospital was a Sprite and then apple juice. They both tasted unusually sweet. Everything she ate and drank for about two weeks tasted bad.

Deputy Sheriff Josh Powell was so sweet to Lisa while she was in the emergency room. He drove to Wiley's Smuteye Grill and purchased her a hamburger and brought it back to her.

Bullock County Circuit Judge Burt Smithart was also very nice to Lisa and said it was the happiest day of his career when she was found.

Bullock County Deputy Chad Faulkner was very helpful. He was so happy she was found. Faulkner was the first person Lisa saw at the hospital. He said, "You don't know how hard we have been searching for you." Lisa felt very comforted by the kindness of everyone in the hospital, which meant so much to her, especially because none of her family was there yet. Lisa remained in the emergency room for about four hours.

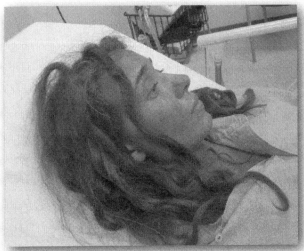

Lisa Theris in Bullock County Hospital Emergency Room shortly after being found.

Lisa took a bubble bath at the hospital for the first time in twenty-five days. Her first bath was painful because of the open cuts and scratches on her body. Then she stood to rinse her hair and was extremely weak, and it was difficult to stand long enough to finish washing her hair.

Lisa looked at herself in the mirror at the hospital and could not believe it was her. She stared in the mirror for a long time. She appeared very thin and bony, and her skin was very dark from being exposed to sunlight.

Lisa said all the doctors and nurses were sweet and helpful. Dr. Morris Cochran inspected all her wounds and released her.

Lisa cried for the first time when her father arrived at the emergency room to pick her up.

Bullock County law enforcement escorted Mr. Theris as he drove Lisa home to Louisville, Alabama. When Lisa arrived at her home, several of her family members had driven from Mobile to meet her, including her mother; her brothers Eman, Rob, and Will; her sister Lizzy; her sister-in-law Eleni; and her nephew Vassilli. Everyone rejoiced.

The Theris Family at Eman's wedding

Dr. Morris Cochran Treats Lisa in the Emergency Room

Dr. Morris Cochran, who specializes in emergency medicine and family medicine, often works in the Bullock County Hospital Emergency Room in Union Springs, Alabama.

He treated Lisa the day she was found and taken to the hospital after being in the woods for twenty-five days. Dr. Cochran graduated from medical school in 1986. He is sixty-three years old and has three daughters. He said when he first saw Lisa's skin it was very dark; he wasn't sure if it was dark from being dirty or from being in the sun for such a long period of time. After showering at the hospital, Lisa's skin was still dark from being tanned by sunlight. Seeing her in that condition reminded Dr. Cochran of going camping for three days with his daughters in Yosemite Park in California. After three days, his daughters thought they had a tan, but they were actually just dirty.

Dr. Cochran first ran a blood test to determine whether Lisa's kidneys were functioning properly. She could not urinate while at the hospital but was able to later that night after she was home. For several weeks, each time she urinated, it was very painful. Lisa was also constipated for about five days. She took magnesium citrate to help with that problem.

The blood test taken by Dr. Cochran revealed her creatinine levels were high. He said her legs were "eaten up" by insects, but he saw no infection or infantigo. She had been drinking water from a stream, which can cause giardia, a waterborne microscopic parasite that causes diarrhea. He gave her Flagyl, an antibiotic, to help treat giardia just in case she had it. He noticed Lisa was extremely dehydrated and gave her three liters of fluid intravenously. He knew her skin—the largest organ a person has—had shut down and was in lifesaving mode.

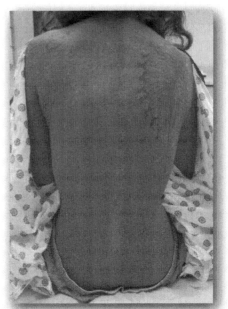

Lisa Theris' back hours after being found.

While in lifesaving mode, her nervous system didn't send signals of pain. Once she was rehydrated, her body slowly started working properly. Her nerves were kick-started, along with the blood vessels that had not been working, and this caused Lisa to start feeling pain again.

That was a great thing for her body, but it was extremely painful, and she itched terribly. The nonstop itching lasted for about two months. Dr. Cochran said, based on statistics, when a person is missing for twenty-five days, they are usually dead. He said it was amazing how the human body could survive and that Lisa was tough. He said the only thing Lisa requested while in the emergency room was to have her hair washed, but it was so matted and tangled, the nurse said she would need to have a professional wash it.

Dr. Cochran said, "A lot of miracles took place, and she did a lot of things right in order to survive. Getting away from the wrong people was the first thing she did right. Finding a water source was another thing. She was lucky the berries and mushrooms she ate were not poisonous." He said some mushrooms can shut down a person's kidneys and kill a person almost instantly.

Dr. Cochran felt the most important thing for Lisa was to reunite her with her father. He did not want to keep her in the hospital, because he felt it would be better emotionally and physically for her to be home with her family. Dr. Cochran remembers saying, "Get her dad on the phone." Once Lisa's dad was on the phone, Dr. Cochran told him, "Come get your baby." The next day Dr. Cochran called Lisa at home to check on her. He said in the emergency room he often sees terrible things, but to see Lisa reunited with her father "recharged him for months."

Survival/Evasion/
Resistance and Escape

• • •

RETIRED COMMAND SERGEANT MAJOR (CSM) Gene Nelson, who ranks E-9 in the US Army Infantry, is very knowledgeable about survival in extraordinary conditions.

CSM Nelson taught SERE (survival, evasion, resistance, and escape) classes at Fort Rucker, a US Army base in Alabama, from 1973 to 1975.

He later attended jungle survival school in the Republic of Panama and overwater survival training at Pensacola Naval Air Force Station in Pensacola, Florida. He served the United States in the Vietnam War.

Nelson had insight on how Lisa's body had survived for twenty-five days. He analyzed the experience of being lost in the woods for that length of time, and reviewed photographs of Lisa's body taken in the emergency room after she found her way out of the woods.

He explained that ketosis is a normal metabolic process in the human body. When the body does not have enough glucose for energy, the body burns stored fats instead. This results in a build-up of acids called ketones within the body. A person's body relies on stored fat when there is no food to eat. Once the body burns all the fat, the body begins to burn muscle. The human body has a difficult time burning muscle into energy, so when a person begins to survive on burning muscle tissue, he or she will soon starve to death. An average person can live three days with no water and twenty-one days with no food.

Becoming disoriented is one of the biggest threats to survival. A person may begin to think irrationally. A person's mind can quickly become disengaged from reality, and his or her logical way of thinking can "come and go."

A major factor in Lisa's ability to survive for the unusually long period of time was the fact that she was able to get drinking water from the South Fork Cowikee Creek.

As Lisa slept in the woods, she had no protection from bugs, insects, and spiders. She pulled ticks that were sucking blood from her body. It is likely that many other ticks probably naturally fell off her body after they were full of blood. An unprotected body in a wooded area becomes a good food source for insects and bugs and can have reactions from vegetation, stings, bug bites, and more.

Retired CSM Nelson said, based on the pictures taken of Lisa's body after being found, it looked like she was very close to dying. He believes she could have survived only a few more days.

Recovery

• • •

INITIALLY, LISA WAS SO HAPPY to be home, and she thought her experience would not have a long-time effect. But as time passed, she noticed that the physical effects are not as bad as the emotional effects. She has always thought of herself as a strong person, but admits this experience has taken a toll on her emotionally. She has always had problems with anxiety, but since being lost, it has become much worse. Sometimes while at home, which is the place she feels the safest, she will have to sleep with a knife clutched in her hand in order to sleep. She randomly cries uncontrollably for no reason. Her psychiatrist told her this is often caused by traumatic experiences when a person's brain unconsciously remembers bad things that have happened. Everyone who knew Lisa before she was lost knew that she would almost never cry. Now the tears just come. She believes one day she will fully recover and be back to her old self, but she doesn't feel it will be anytime soon.

Lisa Theris, Joanne Theris and Lizzy Theris

It took Lisa about four weeks to somewhat recover physically from her experience. The first few weeks, Lisa needed a lot of bed rest. Her entire body hurt even when just lying down. She could barely walk, and her entire body itched almost nonstop. The itching was the worst part of her recovery.

She went to see Dr. Amanda Day, a dermatologist in Dothan, Alabama, for her skin. She told Lisa all the bites would go away, but she would have to get used to the scars, because they would probably always be there. She also told Lisa not to shave her legs or go in the sun for a few months. Dr. Day recommended that Lisa use antibiotic ointment on her cuts and scratches. Lisa's legs will have scars for the rest of her life from various bug bites and from being scratched by thorns and stickers. Lisa has always liked wearing dresses, but now when she wears a dress she feels self-conscious because she thinks people are staring at the scars.

Dr. Leonard Smolinski is a licensed professional counselor located in Ozark, Alabama. Lisa has been visiting his office once a week. He has been using eye movement desensitization and reprocessing (EMDR) to help her bring back her memory from the traumatic experience and learn to cope with it. Eye movement desensitization and reprocessing (EMDR) is a fairly new, nontraditional type of psychotherapy. It's growing in popularity, particularly for treating posttraumatic stress disorder (PTSD), which often occurs after experiences such as military combat, physical assault, rape, or car accidents. Lisa's visits with Dr. Smolinski have greatly helped her recover from the traumatic experience and helped her remember more about the time she was lost.

A doctor located in Ozark, Alabama, tested Lisa for Lyme disease. The test results were neither positive nor negative, but the doctor recommended that Lisa take antibiotics for Lyme disease as a precautionary measure. That doctor also said Lisa tested low in iron, so she began taking iron pills. She also tested positive for mononucleosis.

Lisa was still having numbness in her hands and legs, so a doctor in Dothan, Alabama, requested an MRI. The results of the MRI showed bulging disks in Lisa's neck and lower back. She believes the bulging disks were a result of her automobile accident on July 9, 2017, just nine days before she was lost in the woods.

Lisa spent a lot of time eating and hydrating while recuperating. She gained twenty pounds in the first two weeks. She and her father spent three days untangling her hair. She put conditioners and oils on her hair to try to get the tangles out. It was tangled so badly that Lisa wanted to cut it all off, but her father talked her out of it.

Lisa's twenty-seven-year-old sister, Lizzy, took off work for a week and helped Lisa's mom care for her. She would help Lisa get to the restroom and get dressed, dispense her medicine, and rub ointment on Lisa's cuts and scratches. She would fix her meals, warm blankets in the dryer, and tuck them in around Lisa. Due to her weight loss, Lisa had a hard time staying warm. Lizzy was protective of Lisa and handled her Facebook messages and phone calls so Lisa could recuperate. Lisa said Lizzy was her guardian angel.

Lisa Theris and Lizzy Theris

Emotionally she had a lot of ups and downs and wasn't quite herself. One time she drove through Midway, Alabama, and began to have a panic attack just from being in the area where she had been lost. After driving about thirty more minutes to her home, when she entered her home, her mom noticed she was shaking. She had to sit on their couch for a while to calm down. She sometimes has flashbacks of the dreadful days she spent in the woods, which causes Lisa to have anxiety issues. The stress of being lost in the woods for twenty-five days took a toll on her body, physically and emotionally.

Friends and Family Give Reflections

• • •

SEVERAL OF LISA'S FRIENDS AND family members were asked to write comments about her for this book.

WILLIAM THERIS—LISA'S FATHER SPEAKS

Lisa Theris and her father William Theris

To understand how incredibly happy and elated I was when I received the call saying, "Your daughter has been found," you would have to know how incredibly sad and dark I had been prior to that call.

Will and Bob came up from Mobile to help me look for Lisa while Mom was up in Boston helping her daughter Becky with her newborn, and everybody we talked to—police, friends of Lisa's, and so on—just pointed to the same thing: that she had been killed.

Another girl had disappeared a year ago in the same area, never to be heard from again. Well, we were determined that this was not going to happen to our Lisa. If the police could not find out within the law, well, we were determined to do whatever it took to find her or her body.

I thought, *God help me!!!* I thought dark thoughts, dark thoughts. It was like living in a bad dream with my heart broken and my mind shattered; I was in a zombie-type state.

I had been trying to keep my wife as uninformed as possible, but she finally cornered me on the phone and asked me to tell her what I really thought. I have never been able to lie to her. I remember saying, "I think they killed her." We broke down together, and of course she came home right away.

She had to have our son Nate escort her home. The guys Lisa had been with last were in custody charged with burglary, and I also thought they had killed Lisa. I love Lee Wee (as I call her) so much, and it was just unbearable to imagine that she was gone. Lisa is such a sweetheart, but she has also been a real source of gray hair for Mom and me.

Months before she was lost, we were so happy when Lee Wee came home to go back to school. For a while she was doing so well, but then she started hanging out with losers again. She is very smart and has unlimited potential to do great things and to have a great life, but she was making poor decisions.

I wish I had the intuition Becky had the day Lisa was found. Becky told her husband, Dan, that she knew Lisa was alive and would come out of the woods anytime. At that point I was too far gone to even think straight. When my sister Andrea came to help us look for Lisa, she knew we were thinking dark thoughts of revenge. She counseled us to not do anything. She said God would have his way. However, I was still considering taking things into my own hands. I had dark thoughts and a heavy heart.

When I got the call that Lee Wee had been found alive, wow, I had tears again, but this time they were tears of joy. I thanked God and asked Him to forgive me for getting so dark. Our love was back with us. I thank Investigator McClendon in Troy, Alabama, and Investigator Chad Faulkner in Union Springs, Alabama, for all the help and hard work they did in the case. I thank Police Chief Eugene in Louisville, Alabama, for his support.

I am thankful for Judy, who stopped and helped Lisa after she came out of the woods. I thank Judge Smithart, who was at the hospital when Lisa was brought in. He was such a helper and encourager. He also came to our home when we brought Lisa home from the Bullock County Hospital. Dr. Cochran was very helpful while Lisa was in the emergency room. I thank my neighbors, the Helms, for being so sweet and everyone else who helped with prayers and in other ways.

My prayer is that young people and young girls will be helped by Lisa's story. I also pray Lisa—and I—will continue to choose light rather than darkness and that she will use the same tenacity and effort that she used to survive in the woods and apply that force to move forward in a positive way with her life and to avoid bad influences.

We are so happy to have her back. In conclusion, I would like everyone to know how proud I am of my little girl to have been able to survive such a terrible situation that many of us may not have been capable to withstand. I am extremely proud of what a truly remarkable person she is growing up to be.

NATHANIEL THERIS—LISA'S BROTHER SPEAKS

Lisa Theris and Nathaniel Theris

Looking back to that first, fateful day, it's really no wonder that she ended up being God's own sweet patch of hell. It was a beautiful day in spring when Lisa was born, and the Theris family was congregated in a small local hospital facing a problem they had never encountered: what to name the latest addition to the family.

We had just relocated to the South of France, and I had left behind my childhood love named…Lisa Joy. As the discussion heated up on what to name the new baby, my sister Rebecca, who knew my heart, leaned over and whispered into my ear, "Tell Mama!"

I blurted out the girl's name, and the rest is history. I am Nathaniel Theris, age forty, second born to my parents, and I had moved to Rhode Island when news of Lisa's disappearance reached me. Immediately, I felt like it was all bullshit, and that she was probably just off doing her thing and we would hear from her as soon as she surfaced.

When things became dark, after over a week, I began to come to terms with the possibility that something unthinkable might have befallen my little Moonpie. I can't describe the pain and fury that coursed through me, knowing there was nothing I could do to save her.

My parents suffered terribly, especially Dad, who tirelessly searched for his daughter even after everyone was saying she was gone. Nobody should have to give up their baby sister so young; let us hope that this amazing story helps others see what can happen when people let it all go.

I love my sister with all my fierce heart, now and always. *Hailsa!*

Angelina Theris Owens—Lisa's Sister Speaks

Angelina Owens and Lisa Theris

My name is Angelina Theris Owens, and I was thirty-two years old when Lisa disappeared. As Lisa's older sister, I have known her for all of her charmed life.

We have a large family full of love, fourteen strong. I think Lisa being the youngest has always made everyone especially protective of her: our little summer baby, with her brown skin and blue eyes. Her element is fire; there is a passion to her, a magnetism. She has a way of making you feel so special. It's hard to deny her anything. And she has such a strong will. She is always the life of the party.

I don't like to think about the dark days when we thought she was gone. Those were hard times, and all that matters is that we have our Lisa back. There are no words to describe the joy of hugging her again, all skin and bones; she was so small and fragile. All I could think of was holding her close to me and protecting her.

She has a long road ahead of her—her little body needs time to heal—but she has such strength in her. What an amazing woman. It's hard not to be overprotective to the point of being annoying. But she knows if she needs me, I will always be here.

KAYLA MOATES—LISA'S FRIEND SPEAKS

I have been a friend of Lisa's for over ten years. I am twenty-seven and was the same age at the time she went missing. I met Lisa when I was sixteen. She attended the same school I did and was a classmate of my younger brother's. We quickly became close friends and remained so for several years through high school. We were inseparable at this time. Lisa and I were always together during school breaks, spending a lot of our time at Blue Springs State Park in Blue Springs, Alabama. I was drawn to Lisa's personality from the moment I met her.

She was spontaneous yet laid-back, quiet yet sociable. We had the same sense of humor and found a way to laugh and have fun in every situation, even if we were just sitting at home. We would ride ATVs, watch *Purple Rain* (over and over again), and ride around listening to music. I remember we always had an "inside joke" that no one could ever understand. We would look at each other and burst into laughter, because we knew what the other was thinking. She was my best friend; she was the sister I never had. Unfortunately, we grew apart. I had my first child my senior year and was pushed into becoming an adult before I even graduated.

Lisa was still young; she is about three years younger than me. We tried to remain close, but between my job, school, and a new baby, we drifted apart. We would still see each other from time to time or speak with each other via social media throughout the years, but for about five years, our close friendship dissolved.

On July 13, 2017, I received a phone call from Lisa. After about three years of no communication, we finally spoke. She contacted me through a mutual friend of ours. I was so excited to hear from her. Our conversation did not last long, but we agreed to meet up soon. However, I never heard back from her.

I saw on Facebook where people were posting messages, trying to get in touch with her, but I did not know she was missing. On Sunday, July 23, 2017, I started to feel like something bad had happened. I messaged her brother Robert at 4:41 a.m. on Monday, July 24, 2017, to find out what was going on.

That is when I learned that Lisa was actually missing and had been for almost a week. I immediately sent a message to her at 5:00 a.m., pleading for her to get in contact with me as soon as she could. The next few weeks were a nightmare. I could not sleep at night.

I spent most of my time checking Facebook and messaging Robert to see if there were any updates on where she could be. I would find myself hysterically crying at random moments throughout the day and night. I posted to her Facebook page and sent her private messages, hoping she would see them. It's so hard to describe what I felt, but regret was very heavy.

I regretted losing contact with her. I regretted not being there for her and not laughing with her every day. It devastated me to feel that I might not ever see or speak to her again.

When I found out that she might have been in the Midway area, I kept Google Earth pulled up on my phone or on my computer at work. I would just stare at the miles of woods, wondering where she could be.

There was a feeling that pulled at me constantly to go look for her, especially after the police conducted their search for her and found nothing. I just had a feeling that they were looking in the wrong place. The feeling I had was so strong and nagging, and after I had an emotional breakdown on Tuesday, August 8, 2017, my mother and I decided to drive to Midway the following Saturday after I got off work.

On Wednesday, August 9, 2017, I made a plea while I was getting ready for work. I don't know whom I was talking to, but I just remember saying, "Lisa, I am going to come look for you this weekend. Please give us a sign of where you are. Please don't give up." Wednesday and Thursday night, I actually slept. And the night of Friday, August 11, 2017, I had a dream that I was at my old high school, sitting on the bleachers at the football field. I looked down at the seats below me and saw Lisa. I called her name, ran up to her, and started crying, "Where have you been? We have all been looking for you!"

Lisa pulled me to the side near a water fountain and said, "I can't tell you where I have been. They don't want me to say anything; you will have to wait. It will all come out in the news." Then the class bell rang (or I guess that would have been my alarm clock going off), and I woke up.

Saturday, August 12, 2017, was the day my mother and I had planned to go to the Midway area.

After the dream I had the night before, I knew I had to do something. We had no idea where to look, but I thought at least making an effort might give me some peace. I got off work at 2:00 p.m. and headed home to meet up with my mother. As soon as I pulled into our yard and got out of my car, I received a text from Lisa's brother Robert at 2:31 p.m. that read "OMG! Lisa was found alive!" I opened the door to my mother's room and told her we didn't have to go look for Lisa, because she had been found alive.

We both started crying. I had no details on what had happened, where she was found, or what condition she was in. But she was alive!

I could not wait to hear from Lisa after she was found. I tried to give her time, because I knew she had a lot of healing to do and that her family would be soaking up all her love. But I was so ready to see and talk to her.

When I finally saw her in person, I could see she had physically changed somewhat with her weight loss and the scars on her body, but she was still as beautiful as ever, and when she hugged me, I could feel that she was the Lisa I had missed and loved so much! We sat in her bedroom and talked for six hours, just like we used to.

We talked about her experience and the feelings I had while she was missing. We talked about the past and vowed to never grow apart again. So far, we have made good on that vow. I talk to Lisa multiple times every day. I cannot begin to describe the joy I feel now that I have her back in my life.

She is still the same spontaneous yet laid-back, quiet yet sociable friend whom I was once so close with. But I have also learned more about her. Lisa did something that I don't think I would have had the strength to do. Regardless of how and why she ended up in those woods, alone and lost, she survived and made it back to all of us who love her dearly!

I am proud to say Lisa is back to being my best friend, and I look forward to being there for her with whatever life decides to throw her way.

Elizabeth Theris—Lisa's Sister Speaks

My name is Elizabeth Theris, though friends and family call me Lizzy. I am twenty-seven years old, and I am Lisa's older sister. We grew up together and did everything together, even sharing a room until I was, I think, eleven, and she was nine. Growing into young women, we have been roommates, confidantes, and best friends, sharing countless adventures and disasters.

Lisa is a fiery person, a person of extremes. She is quick to laugh, quick to love, and yes, she can be quick to grow angry. I think that is why people are drawn to her. She has an energy about her, a light. She has an uncanny ability to be both a sweet and precious darling whom you want to protect, and a charismatic and slightly intimidating spitfire whom you hope to impress.

I have always thought of her as a very strong person and have never known her to back down for anything or to make herself smaller for anyone. She is fearless, almost past the point of reason, and I worry that this unflinching belief in her own invincibility can and has led her to fall into dangerous situations.

It is difficult to describe what it felt like when Lisa went missing. At the beginning, we were all concerned that we hadn't heard from her but told ourselves that she was off with friends and would be back home any moment. When those friends we assumed she was with started contacting my parents to ask if they had heard from Lisa, concern turned to alarm, and while we still didn't want to admit to ourselves that anything actually bad could have happened, nothing could shake the uneasiness that permeated every moment, every unanswered call and unread message. These things don't happen to us in real life, right? They happen in movies; they happen on the news; they happen to other people.

I suppose we all believe our lives, our realities, are untouchable, safe from the cruel realities of the world. And it was Lisa. Lisa is strong; Lisa is street smart; how could anything possibly have happened to our Lisa? It was inconceivable. Despite our foolish convictions, time went on, days passed, and any new information only reinforced that inconceivable notion in the backs of our heads, the dreaded thought nobody could acknowledge. Toward the end of that awful month, the dilemma was deciding whether to allow ourselves to face that what the facts were telling us was reality or to hold on to hope despite the odds, even if it might mean a harder letdown should the worst turn out to be true.

I was in willful denial. I didn't honestly believe that there was much hope of Lisa still being alive, but neither would I admit to myself that she was gone. I blocked out my thoughts, I stayed distracted, and I cried myself dry every day without acknowledging the reason. Without the incontrovertible evidence of a body, I could continue in my limbo-like state and pretend.

I was on my way to my older brother's house when I received the text from my mom saying that Lisa had been found alive. It would take a far more creative and eloquent mind than mine to find the words to express how we all felt.

The trip to Louisville has never felt longer than that day. That very night, Lisa was brought home from the hospital by my father, escorted by police cars. It was one thing to hear that she was found on the side of the road and that she had been in the woods the entire time; it was another thing completely to see her. She was so frail, completely emaciated, and all bundled up. She was taken straight to the couch to lie down, while we all wept and tried to be near her without making her feel cornered. I attempted to be soothing by gently stroking her leg and was horrified to be told by one of the police officers that I was probably causing her pain, as her entire body was covered in cuts and welts and insect bites. She had just laid there and smiled at us, not even telling me I was hurting her.

Her recovery has been slow and a definite hardship for her, but she is already almost back to her old self. I was lucky enough to be able to take a week off from work after she came back to us and was able to stay with her and help take care of her. Since then, I have gone back when I am able to on the weekends. It has been wonderful watching her get stronger and put more weight on. She will always carry the scars with her and currently has some health complications that still need attention, but you would never know what she has been through from the way she has bounced back. She still has that fire. I always knew she was strong, but to have survived out there all alone, without even being able to see clearly, means she has proven herself far more resilient and strong-willed than anyone could have suspected. I am in awe of her. Having her back in my life, I struggle with realizing that she is now a grown woman. She has always been the baby of the family, the youngest, the darling. Having been so horribly reminded by the fates that we are not immune to the evils of the world, it is hard not to feel anxious about her going out into it once more. Not that I could ever stop her, of course; she would berate for even thinking about it. But seeing what she can do when she is really fighting for something, what could she not accomplish out there, if she set her will to it?

ROBERT THERIS—LISA'S BROTHER SPEAKS

Lisa Theris and her brother Robert Theris

Hi! I am twenty-eight years old, and I have known Lisa all my life. We have always been really close through the years. Our whole family is, really, but Lisa and I lived together for the longest. We went to the same schools and had a lot of the same friends. She was not only my sister, but also my best friend. I was very protective of her and never approved of any of her boyfriends. No one was good enough, in my opinion.

Before I heard she was missing, I could feel that things were not going well in her life. The silence said it all. I had not heard from her in a while, and I knew she was starting to hang around the wrong crowd again. I wanted to talk to her, but it was not that often that I saw her anymore.

So I tried to keep it light and just have fun whenever we did see each other. I knew something was definitely wrong when I got a message from Melissa, an old friend of hers. Melissa knows I don't like her because of the bad influence she has had on Lisa's life, and she would never message me unless it was a life-or-death situation.

She told me no one had heard from Lisa in a week and that they never went more than two days without talking. She told me that the last two people who were with her were Richard and Lee. I was pretty freaked out, and as time went on, I contacted everybody I could. No one had any answers, and everybody had the same story. I didn't know what to think; I wanted to believe she had just wanted to get away from everything and had run away.

But deep in my heart, I knew that was not the case. I did not know these people, and I had no idea what they were capable of. At one point I thought she might have been traded for money and drugs, and I had my mind set for the worst. For the majority of the time she was lost in the woods, we were being completely misled by a man who barely knew Lisa. Lee's roommate, Tenelio, was the closest person we had to the scene; he claimed he had talked to Richard and Lee after the robbery.

He told us that Lee said Lisa was not coming back. By then we all had come to the conclusion that they had murdered Lisa. Those weeks were the darkest days of my life; all I could do was think of her. Even though I had my mind made up that she was gone, I still prayed every night. I begged God to bring her back to us, and I broke down on numerous nights.

I was on my way to face my mother when I received the text message that Lisa had been found alive. I was never so pleasantly surprised in my life. I jumped right in my car and headed straight for the hospital. I received a text from my sister halfway there, and she informed me that Lisa had been released and was home. As I turned around, she sent me a text saying, "Be ready." The text message really worried me; did this mean Lisa was disfigured? Or had lost a body part? When I finally saw Lisa, I shed tears of joy. I wanted to hug her so bad, but she was too weak, and I did not want to hurt her. Although she was weak and feeble, she looked so beautiful to me. Obviously she did not say much, but I just loved being around her.

I lay next to her as she slept, and I was just so thankful to have her back in my life. Now that she is back, I just want to make sure she does not go back to hanging around the wrong people. This was a life-changing story, and clearly God has plans for her. While she was gone, I thought about all that I could have done to have stopped this from happening. I almost lost my sister once, and I do not plan on ever letting this happen again.

WILL THERIS—LISA'S BROTHER SPEAKS

Will Theris and Lisa Theris

I was thirty years old when Lisa went missing. I am her older brother and one of three siblings who grew up with her in her younger years while the older siblings moved out on their own.

Ever since she was a child, she has always been very tough while also extremely charismatic. Even as a toddler, she would hang out with the older ones in the family. One of her greatest blessings and curses was the ability to adapt to any type of people she was around, absorbing everything she witnessed and experienced like a sponge.

And that manifested itself in the year leading up to her disappearance as she began increasingly associating herself with low-lifes who were less friends and more just using her for their own gain. And her lifestyle and personality changed along with it.

A few weeks before her disappearance, Rob, Lizzy, and I (the three youngest siblings) visited home, and Lisa didn't even show up all weekend to see us. It was the first time that had ever happened, and we all agreed it was quite obvious then that something was very wrong.

One fateful night not too long after, we were just returning from the beach and were lounging around having a good time when we got a phone call alerting us she had been missing for five days. Mixed emotions of both grief and anger followed, and several of us took work off to go down to Troy and spend time with our father and try to find any kind of information on what had happened.

While part of me wanted to think optimistically, another part was more and more convinced with every passing day that she was gone. And two instances sealed the deal in my mind. One morning, when we were preparing to bring some of her clothes to the police for dogs to pick up her scent, we got a phone call from a friend who told us as if it were a confirmed fact that her body had been found with a shotgun blast to the face.

After a half-hour period of intense grieving, we got ourselves together enough to make some phone calls to the police stations, and it turned out to be a bogus rumor. Worse yet, we later spoke with a roommate of one of the men Lisa was last seen with, and he told us he was specifically told by his roommate that she was dead and gone.

At that particular point, it seemed so real, and he seemed so convincing. The only thing that sounded fake about the whole thing was that he said Lisa was terrified and submissive to the guy and was as obedient as a dog. And anyone who knows Lisa knows she backs down from no one—no matter the circumstances. We should have paid closer attention to that hint as he turned out to be a mentally broken, compulsive liar who later admitted to police that he had been lying to basically everyone.

Between all the false and misleading information from numerous sources, I had no idea what really happened, but I was convinced she was gone...which is why the day I received the text message that she had been found alive was the most surreal, unbelievable moment of my entire life. All the family from the Mobile area immediately drove up to Louisville.

It was a very strange feeling driving down, knowing the unbelievable had happened, and it didn't even strike me as real until I saw her lying on my parents' couch, living and breathing. In that moment it didn't even matter that she was tiny and shriveled and barely able to speak, it was wonderful just being able to hold her in my arms again, someone I thought I had lost for good.

My main thoughts in the aftermath of this insane situation are how amazed and proud I am of Lisa for somehow surviving such an ordeal. It is nothing short of miraculous that she was able to withstand so many trials and tribulations and hold strong throughout such severe suffering in such terrible conditions. And despite some severe pains and fevers, as well as dramatic weight loss, she's stronger every time I see her, and I have no doubt that she will make a full recovery.

I also hope she takes this experience and uses it as a lesson to be more careful of the types of people she hangs out with. Lisa is a very nonjudgmental person and sometimes allows people into her circle who are not worthy of her presence, which has a lot to do with her rebellious nature. She just seems naturally drawn to trouble, and I really hope that her experience surviving this will give her a new outlook on life regarding the lifestyle she lives and the people she puts her trust in.

Lisa's Thoughts While in the Woods

• • •

In Lisa's Own Words

It is needless to say the thing I thought about most while in the woods was my family. I thought about my four-year-old nephew, whom I would never get to see grow up if I didn't make it out. I imagined my niece and nephew in France growing up and never remembering me.

I had dreadful thoughts of dying in the woods and my parents never finding my body, because at the time no one knew where on earth I was. I felt their minds and hearts would never be put to ease.

I hated the fact that I would never make my family proud. I regretted not spending more time with my dad's family. I really regretted not spending more time with my mother's family, whom I had met only once. I regretted so many choices I had made in my life.

I thought back to my younger years and remembered that my sister Lizzy would often tell me I was invincible. That memory helped keep me going.

I tried to think of the one moment, the exact time, I had made the mistake in my life that led me to this point. You have to keep in mind, when I woke up naked in the woods, I had no memory of how I got to this location or why I had no clothes on.

It was such a strange thing to wake up in a place like that. I thought it must be a nightmare. I kept closing my eyes, thinking it was a dream and all I had to do was make myself wake up. I can't explain the terror I felt when I finally realized this was really happening to me.

From that moment on, I was in complete survival mode. The days and nights were long and hard. At first I would get hungry from time to time and picture the tastes of my favorite foods. I would think about my dad's and brother's cooking. After about the first week, the hunger faded away, and I got used to the feeling of being empty.

But the thirst never went away. It only got worse. At night I would think about all the different drinks I would enjoy when I made it out of that place. I never really drank soda before that happened, but I found myself picturing all the different sodas and how they would taste. I told myself, *When I go home, I will be a new person—a better person, the person I really was deep down before I let the life I was living change me.*

I thought about a lot of things while in the woods, including past relationships and where I would be if I hadn't ended them. I thought anywhere would be better than here. But the only place I really longed to be was home.

Lisa's New Outlook on Life

• • •

Lisa Theris

Lisa Joy Theris does not look down on anyone who uses drugs, no matter whether they are using drugs recreationally or have a drug addiction. Lisa has used drugs recreationally and at times has also been addicted to drugs. Most of the people she knows who use drugs in either way have a hard life.

Most of Lisa's former friends who used drugs have parents who used drugs also, so they were introduced to "the drug life" at a young age. She calls it "the drug life" because if people are using illegal drugs, you better believe their lives have changed. They are in a different circle of people, and they do different things in their free time.

People often become friends with one another just because they like the same drug. Everybody knows everybody in "the drug life." Lisa believes many of these friendships are real. She had people she cared deeply about and still cares deeply about who were fellow drug users. But a lot of people in that condition will steal from their best friends and then get high with them the next day.

People who use drugs every day stop hanging out with friends who don't get high. It is not because the users think friends who don't use drugs are not cool or because the users don't have fun with them; it is because the users are ashamed of their lifestyle, or at least that is how it was for Lisa.

She distanced herself from quite a few real friendships. Luckily for Lisa, she is regaining them now that she is clean. Lisa said, to be honest, it is hard after quitting drugs to get used to a normal life, not only with friends but with anyone.

Lisa still thinks about getting high, but she believes, hopes, and prays she will never touch drugs again after being lost in the woods for twenty-five days. A couple of weeks after getting out of the woods and into her recovery, she went out for the first time to pick up some of her things she had left at a friend's house. Lisa asked another friend at the house if he could touch up her tattoos when her skin healed. He then offered Lisa his drug of choice, ice, and she told him that she was clean.

He respectfully did not use drugs in front of her. Lisa stayed and talked to him and his girlfriend, who also had been Lisa's friend for a while. They asked questions about her being lost in the woods and told her they had been looking for her also. It was not uncomfortable for Lisa to be around the drug users and not use it. She left happy, thinking she could keep her friendships with people who were still using drugs so long as she stayed strong, and they were the right type of friends. During the months after being found, Lisa began to distance herself from almost all her old friends. She believes most of them were just using her to get a ride, get drugs, or other things like that. She was always good hearted and found it difficult to tell people no. She believes they felt uncomfortable hanging around her because she was no longer using drugs. Looking back, she questions herself for being friends with some of them, because they were always stealing from one another, had no ambition, and didn't want to better their lives. Many drug users she knew would spend most of their time each day trying to figure out a way to get high again. They would steal from people they knew, beg family members for money, or pawn anything they owned, and some girls would even have sex for drugs.

It is sad for Lisa to see or hear that some of these people are still in and out of jail, doing the same stuff, and saying they want to change but never changing. Lisa was no different from any other drug user before getting lost in the woods. She would move to a new city and tell herself, "No more drugs." But she would start using alcohol or a different drug. Lisa Joy was an alcoholic at a young age. At an older age, she would wake up with a bottle by the bed, begin drinking, and would not stop drinking until she passed out at night.

Drinking was a part of her everyday life for years. She would drink at work. She would get drunk and make a scene at family functions. Taking pills got Lisa off liquor. Ice got her off pills.

Being in the woods for twenty-five days got her off everything, cold turkey—not by choice, of course.

Lisa wants to find out the details about hypnotherapy. She believes this will be a good thing to do. She still has nightmares about going to sleep in her bed and waking up in the woods. She believes God made sure she got out of the woods for a purpose, though she doesn't know what the purpose is yet.

She has a neighbor in Louisville, Mrs. Lenora Helms, who has been very sweet since Lisa was found. She took clothes to Lisa's house that actually fit, since she had lost so much weight.

A policeman in Louisville whom they call Barney has been very nice as well. They have joked with each other. He said Lisa's story and her experience of being lost in the woods encouraged him to rejoin church and regain his faith, and for that Lisa is thankful. She is attending church and has gone to a Bible study group. No more drugs for Lisa Joy. She will never sell drugs again. She never wants to see drugs or be around drugs. She said she is done with drugs. *Done!*

Lisa appreciates everything so much more since finding her way out of the woods. She is much more cautious and says it is hard to trust anybody.

Lisa is from a big family, and they are really close. She thought about her family much of the time while she was in the woods. She was going through hell in the woods, and her family was too while she was lost. She is very proud of her father for all the things he has done for her family. Lisa said he is selfless and loves them very much. Lisa said her mother has had the biggest influence on her life. She has taught Lisa things about everyday life and is the kindest person she knows.

A close friend, Wayne Williams, gave Lisa a necklace with a bullet pendant and a yellow sapphire on the chain. He said he gave it to her because he believes she is bulletproof.

Lisa said she hopes to go back to school someday and earn a degree so she can make her parents proud.

She thanks God for the experience of being lost in the woods, because now she is finally clean, and it is the freest feeling she has ever had. She prays that maybe some drug users will get something out of her story, and maybe it will do some good in their lives. There is never a better time than right now to change your life, to be free.

Lisa Theris a few months after being found

Lisa Theris a few months after being found

About the Authors

• • •

JOHNNY ADAMS AND HIS SISTER, Kim Adams Graham, were born and raised in Union Springs, Alabama. Together, they own and operate the *Union Springs Herald*, where Adams serves as the newspaper editor and Graham serves as the newspaper publisher.

Adams holds a bachelor of science from Troy University and earned his juris doctor from the Birmingham School of Law. He serves as a Bullock County Commissioner, a board member of the Bullock County E911 Board, and a member of the Alabama Press Association Journalism Foundation Board.

Adams is married to Shirley Rowland Adams. They have two adult daughters, Abby and Leslie. Adams enjoys church, his family, and learning about new technology. He is the author of *Success: Why Wait Any Longer?*

Kim Adams Graham, who is married to Tim Graham, owns Adams Pecan and Adams Florist in addition to the *Union Springs Herald*. She is the author of *Pearls of Wisdom* and *The Pecan Cookbook*.